guide to Barcelona

Text, photographs, design, lay-out and
printing completely created by
the technical department of
EDITORIAL ESCUDO DE ORO S.A.

www.eoro.com
e-mail: editorial@eoro.com

Editorial Escudo de Oro, S.A.

INTRODUCTION

Barcelona, capital of Catalonia, is situated on a site bathed by the Mediterranean sea and bordered at either end by the Llobregat and Besòs river deltas. It is surrounded by the Sierra de Collserola, whose highest point is Mount Tibidabo (512 m). Another of the mountains looking down on the city is Montjuïc, rising over the sea. Barcelona is made up of the old centre, the Eixample district (built during the period of expansion in the 19th century) and the peripheral areas enveloping the first two zones.

The climate here is typically Mediterranean, with hot summers and mild winters and annual average temperatures of 16°C.

The enormous economic strength of this large, dynamic city comes in part from its privileged geographical position, added to which is the traditionally enterprising nature of its inhabitants. Its continuous expansion perfectly reflects the desire to perfect the city and the outward-looking character of the Barcelonans. A cosmopolitan metropolis, Barcelona affords visitors a warm, sincere welcome.

A veritable crossroads, Barcelona both takes to its heart and transmits cultural and artistic currents of all types and is an inexhaustible source of creative power. Proud of its culture and traditions, Barcelona jealously conserves its signs of identity (language, culture, folklore) and projects them beyond its frontiers. Barcelona's organisation of the 1992 Olympics, considered by many to be best in the history of the Games, provided the chance, eagerly seized, of regenerating this dynamic city and launching it confidently towards the future.

HOW TO USE THIS GUIDE

This guide is divided into itineraries, classified into three categories (***), (**) and (*) according to both the historic and artistic importance of the monuments included in each and the picturesque qualities and atmosphere of the areas visited. In the same way, the buildings visited in each itinerary are classified as essential (***), recommended (**) or interesting (*).

Next to the rating for each itinerary is indicated the best time to follow it: in the morning (M), in the afternoon/evening (A) or the entire day (M and A), though visitors are also recommended to check the length of each, as some (itineraries 3, 4, 7 and 8, for example) cover long distances.

We hope that these indications and recommendations will enable those on just a short visit to see the most outstanding sights in the city.

HISTORIC BACKGROUND

The varied, eventful history of Barcelona began almost 4,000 years ago with the first settlements on the slopes of Montjuïc. These were built by the Layetans, who grew crops, kept cattle and, thanks to their geographic position, were able to trade with the Greeks, Punics and Romans. However, it was with the Roman occupation that the city really began to take form. Once the conquest of the Peninsula was completed with the successful campaigns against the Cantabrians and the Asturs, Emperor Augustus carried out administrative reforms and built roads which led to the construction of various cities. It was in around 15 BC, that Iulia Augusta Paterna Faventia Barcino came into being, a city built on a small hill known as Mons Taber, on the site of what is now the Gothic Quarter. In around the 4th century AD, the growing city was protected by an encircling wall, giving Barcelona strategic importance and affording a solid defence against barbarian attacks.

With the decline of the Roman Empire came the invasion of the Germanic tribes, and in the year 415 the Visigoth ruler Ataulfo made Barcelona the capital of his kingdom, though this status was later lost as the Visigoth capital was transferred first to Tolosa and one century later to Toledo.

In the 8th century, the city came under Moorish rule, remaining so for almost one hundred years until it was reconquered by the Franks in the year 801, when the lands south of the Pyrenees formed the Marca Hispánica, the frontier of Islam with the Christian world. For several centuries, Barcelona was

Marble bust of the empress Agrippina (1st century). History Museum of Barcelona.

Sculpture of Diana. History Museum of Barcelona.

constantly under threat due to the conflict between Moors and Christians. The outstanding historical personage of this period of Barcelona's history was Wilfred, known as "the Hairy", founder of the Catalan dynasty of the counts of Barcelona in the year 878. In 985, the city was destroyed by the Saracen troops of Almanzor and Count Borrell II, grandson of Wilfred, left defenceless against the Moorish onslaught, broke all ties with the Carolingian empire, making Barcelona the capital of a new independent state. This move heralded the beginning of a flourishing period for the city, which asserted its supremacy over all the other Catalan countships. The city expanded towards the sea, beyond the old Roman walls, the new buildings clustering, for the most part, around one of the first Christian churches to be constructed here, Santa Maria del Mar.

After the union of Catalonia and Aragon in the 13th century, King Jaume I founded the first representative institutions, the "Consell de Cent" (a council of 100 notables elected by the people) and "Les Corts" (the Courts). At the same time, Jaume began to exert his naval power, conquering Majorca

Barcelona paleo-christian basilica mural (6th century). History Museum of Barcelona.

and Valencia. His successor, Pere III, the Great, added Sicily and Sardinia to the reign. Such expansion greatly increased trade and the wealth of the capital, and Barcelona became one of the great Mediterranean powers of the

Christian tomb mosaic (5th century). History Museum of Barcelona.

Mural of the military expedition of Peter the Great (13th century). History Museum of Barcelona.

period. In order to foster this supremacy, the Royal Boatyards ("Drassanes") were built, the largest medieval boatyards now conserved in the world. Towards the end of the 15th century, with the rise to power of the Catholic Monarchs, the capital was transferred

Illuminated page from the "Commentaries on Social Customs and Practices" (Jaume Marquilles, 15th century). History Museum of Barcelona.

from Barcelona to Toledo. Later, during the War of Spanish Succession (1710-14), Barcelona gave its support ot Archduke Charles of Austria against the other candidate to the throne, Philip V of the House of Bourbon, the eventual victor. The last episode in the war was the 13-month siege of Barcelona by French and Spanish troops. On 11 September 1714, the Bourbon army occupied the city and Philip V suppressed Catalonia's independent institutions, prohibiting the use of the Catalan language and ensuring control of the city by building the Ciutadella fortifications. From 1808 to 1813, Barcelona was occupied by the French army and the process of economic and social development came to a standstill during this period. Nevertheless, the surging population growth of the 19th century led to the demolition of the city walls, which were hampering the city's expansion, in 1859. The Cerdà Plan, one of the first rational designs for urban development in Europe was adopted for the construction of the "Eixample" (expansion) beyond the old walls. This plan entailed the construction of blocks of houses forming a regular grid pattern from the city centre to the beginning of the mountain.

One of the most outstanding transformations of the city came about on the occasion of the Universal Exhibition in 1888. The site chosen for this great event was the Ciutadella Park, where such important buildings as the palaces of industry and fine arts were erected. The Arch of Triumph was constructed as the entrance to the exhibition site. The Universal Exhibition was a clear indication of the city's desire to surpass itself and take its rightful place on the international map by merit of its economic development, social vitality and political dynamism.

The beginning of the 20th century was marked by social upheaval. The radical division of the city into working class and bourgeois caused great inequalities resulting in a vicious circle of attack and reprisal. However, in 1929, during the dictatorship of Primo de Rivera, who had deposed the monarchy, Barcelona was once more the venue for an important international event which stimulated the renovation and modernisation of the city. The staging of the 1929 Universal Exhibition led to the opening of the Metro, the transformation of Montjuïc (including the creation of the famous illuminated fountain) and the construction of various other important buildings.

The Generalitat (autonomous government of Catalonia) established its seat in Barcelona in 1931, and during the Spanish Civil War the city formed part of the Republican side. During the subsequent Franco dictatorship, massive immigration from the country to the city and the enormous economic development of the 1960s transformed the entire country. In 1975, the monarchy, democracy and Catalan autonomy were restored to mark the beginning of another dynamic phase in the history of Barcelona. This new impulse led to the city taking on another great challenge: the organisation of the 1992 Olympic Games. In preparation for the Games, Barcelona underwent the greatest urban transformation of its entire history, demolishing the physical barriers which had denied it contact with its coastline, constructing new infrastructures and becoming more competitive. Barcelona today is a cosmopolitan metropolis, modern, dynamic and ready to take on future challenges.

Palau Sant Jordi.

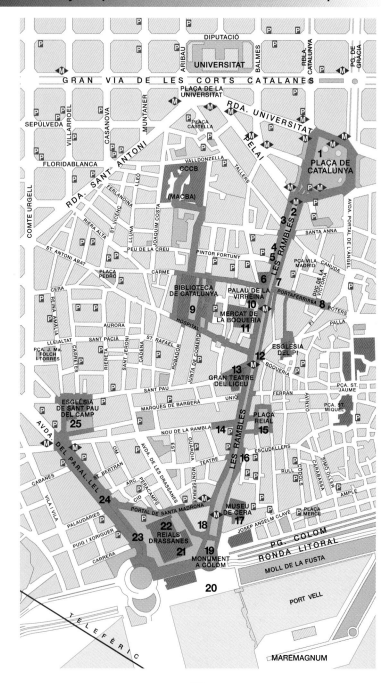

ITINERARY 1 (***) (M)

The first itinerary we propose will take us down one of the best-loved and most famous thoroughfares in Barcelona: the unique, colourful Ramblas. From the very centre of the city, we will slowly and eventfully approach one of the great attractions of modern Barcelona: its sea front, described later on in the pages of this guide.

1.- Catalunya Square (**). 2.- The Ramblas (***). 3.- Canaletes Fountain (***). 4.- Poliorama Theatre (**). 5.- Compañía de Tabacos de Filipinas (*). 6.- Bethlehem Church (***). 7.- Moja Palace (*). 8.- Portaferrissa Street (**). 9.- Former Hospital de la Santa Creu (**). 10.- Virreina Palace (***). 11.- Boqueria Market (***). 12.- Pla de l'Os (**). 13.- Liceu Opera House and Theatre (***). 14.- Güell Palace (***). 15.- Royal Square (***). 16.- Teatre Square (*). 17.- Wax Museum (**). 18.- Santa Mònica Art Centre (*). 19.- Monument to Columbus (***). 20.- Port (**). 21.- Maritime Museum (**). 22.- Royal Shipyards (***). 23.- Medieval walls (**). 24.- Paral·lel Avenue (**). 25.- Church of Sant Pau del Camp (**).

This first walk begins in **Catalunya Square (1)**, nerve centre of the city and the starting-point of most of its communications. The square is flanked on all sides by splendid buildings now the headquarters of banks or important stores and shopping centres (such are El Corte Inglés and "El Triangle" shopping centre), and the central plaza is surrounded by several large fountains. In one corner is the recently-unveiled monument to

Aerial view of Catalunya Square.

Catalunya Square.

Monument dedicated to Francesc Macià, the work of Josep M. Subirachs.

Francesc Macià, former president of the Generalitat of Catalonia.

Originally, **the Ramblas (2)** was nothing more than a river-bed delineating the outer limits of the 13th-century city walls. A promenade was formed running parallel th the walls, which were perforated with various entrances such as the gates of Santa Anna, Portaferrissa, Boqueria and Drassanes. With time, these walls ceased to serve their defensive function and were destroyed and the outer zones, including the Ramblas, developed to become part of the city. All along the Ramblas were built houses, hospitals and colleges, forming the splendid promenade we see today with the planting of trees and the installation of benches in the 18th century. The various sections of the Ramblas have different names, the stretch beginning in Catalunya Square being known as **Rambla de Canaletes**. This is followed by the **Rambla dels Estudis**, the **Rambla de les Flors, Rambla Caputxins** and the **Rambla de Santa Mònica.** Along the centre are stalls selling flowers, animals and newspapers and magazines, whilst further down are pavement cafés and stands selling craftwork, as well as street performers, usually surrounded by curious onlookers, Tarot card readers and portrait artists.

As full as the Ramblas is of human life and activity, it is also full of historic and artistic treasures. Firstly, for example, we come to the **Canaletes Fountain (3)**, one of the most symbolic monuments on the Rambla This is a 19th-century iron fountain which has been witness to many of the outstanding events in the city's recent history. The fountain has four outlets

Romanesque church, Santa Anna, located near to Catalunya Square.

Canaletes Fountain.

and is crowned by the brackets of four streetlights. According to local legend, all those who drink from the Font de Canaletas are destined to return to Barcelona.

As we continue along the Rambla, we come to the **Reial Acadèmia de Ciències i Arts** (right), since 1929 the **Poliorama Theatre (4)**. The Academy of Science and Art was founded in the 18th century, after the disappearance of the Estudi General, a Jesuit college which gave its name to the Rambla dels Estudis. It was here that degree courses were given at the time when there were no universities in Barcelona. Further down, on the same side, is the **Compañía de Tabacos de Filipinas (5)**, a typical 19th-century bourgeois building

Flower and newspaper stalls in the Ramblas.

The Ramblas.

"Live statue" in the Ramblas.

The Ramblas: Bird vending stall.

dating back to 1880. Next to it is the lovely **Bethlehem Church (6)**, formerly a Jesuit monastery and one of the few Baroque monuments in Barcelona. It began to be built in 1681 and was finally completed in 1732. Over the entrance is a relief depicting the Nativity and on the main front, giving onto Carme Street, are statues of Saint Ignacius of Loyola and Saint Francis of Borja. The statue adorning the front facing the Rambla is of Saint John the Baptist. The interior of the church is formed by a nave with numerous side chapels. The sumptuous decoration of the interior was completed in 1855 by destroyed by fire in 1936. Every Christmas the church houses an interesting exhibition of cribs.

On the other side of the Ramblas is the **Moja Palace (7)**, marking the beginning of **Portaferrissa Street (8)** an important shopping street. The palace was for a time home to the poet Verdaguer, under the patronage of the marquises of Comillas, who had bought the building from the Moja family.

Bethlehem Church.

Moja Palace.

Mural and fountain in Portaferrissa Street.

Patio of the old Hospital de la Santa Creu.

To come to our next port of call, the **Former Hospital de la Santa Creu (9)**, we must leave the Rambla for a short time, taking either Carme Street or Hospital Street. These former hospital buildings date back orginally to the 15th century, though not completed until the 18th. The hospital was set up to join together all the health care centres in Barcelona, and continued to function as a hospital until 1926, when the Santa Creu i Sant Pau clinics were opened in the Eixample district. The buildings now house a number of important cultural institutions, including the **Library of Catalonia** and the **Institute of Catalan Studies**. The former hospital features a number of huge rooms in Gothic and Baroque style, decorated with ceramic works, such as the **Convalescent Home** with its unique porticoed courtyard. There are also Neoclassical creations, such as the **College of Surgery** (1761), designed by Ventura Rodríguez Tizón, now seat of the **Medical Academy**.

Close by, around the Angels square are situated three large centres dedicated to the new trends, in their most varied forms of expression: the **Museum of Contemporary Art of Barcelona (MACBA)**, the original building was planned by Richard Meier and first opened its doors in 1995; the **Convent dels Àngels**, a gothic building that has been the headquarters of the cultural body FAD since 1999, with regard to design; and the **Contemporary Culture Centre of Barcelona (CCCB)**, situated in the old 18th century Casa de la

MACBA (Museum of Contemporary Art of Barcelona).

Manning Patio, CCCB (Contemporary Culture Centre of Barcelona).

Virreina Palace.

Caritat. This cultural centre has operated since 1994 as a gallery for seasonal exhibitions.

Returning to the Rambla, going down towards the sea we come to the **Virreina Palace (10)**. An 18th-century Baroque building, its Rococo decoration makes continuous references to the twelve months of the year. The front is flanked by sculptures by Gargallo. The palace was commissioned by the Viceroy of Peru, Manuel de Amat i Junyent, as his residence here, but he died shortly after work was completed, and it was finally his widow who established herself here for a time (hence the name of the palace). The Palace de la Virreina is considered a model of perfection among 18th-century Catalan civil

Modernist shop on the corner of the Ramblas and Petxina Street.

Pla de l'Os or the Boqueria: mosaic by Miró.

architecture and was declared a Historic-Artistic Monument of National Interest in 1941.

A little farther down the Rambla, we come to the popular **Boqueria Market (11)** (or of Sant Josep). The market, originally opened in the 18th century, is housed in an interesting Modernist construction with transparent iron and glass roof. This, and the bustling atmosphere inside make it well worth pausing here for a moment. We now come to the stretch known as the Rambla dels Caputxins, where we can admire and even walk over the **Pla de l'Os or the Boqueria (12)**,

Announcement in the Boqueria Market and dragon, Bruno Quadros House, in the Pla de l'Os.

Liceu Opera House and Theatre.

Café de l'Opera.

by Miró (1977), a mosaic work set into the pavement and dedicated to the nearby market.

Our next stop is one of the traditional homes of Catalan culture and the pride of the people of Barcelona. The **Liceu Opera House and Theatre (13)** was first opened in 1847 but unfortunately the principal rooms were destroyed in a fire in 1994, the facade giving on to the Rambla being all that could be saved. After an intense period of rebuilding, which included enlarging the building on the south side, the Liceu was reopened at the end of 1999. The "Liceu" was built in the 19th century on the site of a former convent of Descalced Trinitarians in a style embodying the splendour of the Catalan bourgeoisie of that period. The first fire occurred in 1861, causing serious damage and requiring rehabilitation at the hands of the architect Mestres, though it was later completely remodelled by Pere Falqués, who had taken part in its original construction. These two fires were not the only mishap to occur to the building, however, as in 1893 an anarchist threw two bombs into the stalls. Only one actually exploded, killing 20 people. Nevertheless, the Liceu overcame its turbulent history to become one of the best-known opera houses in the world. Its ample auditorium and five storeys seated 3,500, a capacity only bettered by La Scala in Milan. The interior featured a splendid central ceiling, considered a masterpiece of 19th-century Catalan interior decorative art. Opposite the theatre is the **Café de l'Opera**, which still conserves all the air of its early-20th-century origins.

In nearby Nou de la Rambla Street is another architectural jewel: the **Güell Palace (14)**, designed by Gaudí. The interior features mosaic-lined fireplaces and the entrance innovative

Güell Palace.

parabolic arches. This palace was commissioned by Count Güell to serve as the setting for his social reunions and as a residence for guests. The mighty work was completed in 1888, having taken just two years, coinciding with the opening of the Universal Exhibition. The Palau Güell was declared a Historic-Artistic Monument of National Interest in 1969, whilst in 1984 UNESCO listed it in its Catalogue of Patrimony of Humanity.

Güell Palace roof.

Royal Square.

Royal Square: street lamp designed by Gaudí and the Tres Glòries fountain.

Down towards the blue Mediterranean we continue, pausing to discover on the left the **Royal Square (15)**, one of the city's most emblematic spaces. This lively square is flanked on all sides by tall buildings, constructed over the site of a Capuchins' monastery, supported by porticoes between whose archways are pavement cafés and bars. In the centre is the Fountain of the Tres Glòries and lamp posts with six brackets, also designed by Gaudí. The square presents a "collage" of people to defy the imagination: one might see anything here. Recently, many artists and the like have bought and refurbished flats overlooking the square, which on one side connects with Ferran Street, giving it a somewhat intellectual air. On Sunday mornings, a stamp and coin market is held here.

Monument dedicated to the playwright and poet Frederic Soler, "Pitarra".

Entrance to the Wax Museum.

In **Teatre Square (16)**, containing the **monument to the writer Pitarra**, by Pere Falqués and Agustí Querol, stands the 16th-century **Principal Theatre**, Barcelona's first theatre and which still conserves its original front. Built thanks to special authorisation from King Philip II, the theatre was originally used for rehearsing productions at the Liceu, reopened as a theatre in 1999. Opposite the Principal is a number of buildings forming part of Barcelona's newest university, the **Pompeu Fabra University**.

In the Rambla de Santa Mónica is one of the museums dearest to the hearts of the people of Barcelona, the **Wax Museum (17)** Located in the tiny Passatge de la Banca, this museum contains over 300 wax statues. It is housed in a lovely 19th-century building and was founded in

Room in the Wax Museum.

1973 by the film director Enrique Alarcón, who also used his knowledge of the film industry to create sets appropriate to the period to which the figures represented belong.

Opposite the Wax Museum is the new **Santa Mònica Art Centre (18)**, housed in the dependencies of the former convent of the same name, dating back to 1626. The building was abandoned in the 19th century due to its ruinous state, but was recovered and refurbished by architects Piñón and Viaplana.

Those wishing to discover a different side to Barcelona are recommended to visit the **Raval district**, which spreads out from the right-hand side of the Ramblas and conceals many interesting pubs, clubs and bars.

Our tour of the Ramblas ends in **Portal de la Pau,** in the centre of which rises the **Monument to Columbus (19)** This was built for the 1888 Universal Exhibition and is crowned by a statue of the discoverer of America pointing the way to the New World. The column is 87 metres high and the statue 7 metres high. A lift takes visitors to a gallery just below the statue, commanding fine views of the entire city.

Nearby is the **Port of Barcelona (20)**,

Santa Mònica Art Centre.

Monument to Columbus.

Portal de la Pau, Barcelona Royal Nautical Club and Maremàgnum.

Gate of Europe, drawbridge in the port of Barcelona.

from where the popular "Golondrinas" and other boats offer trips to see another facet of Barcelona: its sea front, recovered and renovated on the occasion of the 1992 Olympic Games. And also opposite the monument to Columbus the **Pasarela de Mar** stretches out, an attractive wood bridge raised over the sea harbour, that leads you to the **Maremàgnum** leisure centre (see Itinerary 3).

Pleasure boats known as "Golondrinas". Cable railway and the Barceloneta quarter.

This first itinerary could be brought to an end suitably with a visit to the **Maritime Museum (21)**, which contains a number of spectacular boats and a collection of interesting pieces referring to the sea-faring history of the entire country, particularly the 14th and 15th centuries. The museum occupies the three huge halls of the **Drassanes or Royal Shipyards (22)**.

Aerial view of the port of Barcelona.

Three views of the shipyards, today the site of the Maritime Museum: exterior, inner room and the galley of John of Austria.

type in the world. In these Drassanes is one of the gateways to the old **Medieval walls (23)**, the only remaining section of which stand nearby in a gardened area. They were discovered in 1939, during the latest reconstruction of the shipyards. The entire site was declared a Historic-Artistic Monument of National Interest in 1976.

Next to these shipyards is the starting-point of **Paral·lel Avenue (24)**, one of the most famous thoroughfares of Barcelona, one which for years was the centre of entertainment and theatre in the city. "Paral·lel", whose name is due to the fact that

This was where, for centuries, some of the most important boats were built, some of them taking part in such important historic battles as Lepanto or Tunis. The shipyards were built in the 14th century by Arnau Ferrer and are now considered the largest and best-conserved of their

Medieval walls.

Paral·lel Avenue: "El Molino" before it was closed in 1999, and a monument dedicated to Raquel Meyer, varieties artist.

Arnau Theatre.

its course coincides with Parallel 41-44, signified for many their first contact with the variety show. The avenue is the site of some of the oldest and best-loved theatres in Barcelona, such as the **Arnau Theatre** and **Apolo**, though the most famous of all, without doubt, **El Molino**, which first opened its doors to the public in 1913 although it closed down as stage in 1999. Besides this music hall, Avenue Paral·lel now contains others, as well discotheques and nightclubs, all installed in former variety theatres.

We may well be surprised, then, to find in the middle of this centre of nightlife, to find such a lovely building as the **Church of Sant Pau del Camp (25)**, founded as a Benedictine abbey in the 10th century and a splendid example of 11th-century (and earlier, as it contains the tombstone of Wilfred II, dated 912) Catalan Romanesque art. The church, entered from Sant Pau Street, is surrounded by lovely gardens and its front features series of Lombard arches and the remains of fortifications. Inside, the church has a Greek cross groundplan and the cloisters are the only Catalan Romanesque work with trefoiled arches. Its name (Saint Paul in the Field) is due to the fact that it originally stood among cultivated fields. As far back as 1879, the church was declared of National Interest, though it was seriously damaged during the "Setmana Tràgica" ("tragic week") of 1909.

Church of Sant Pau del Camp and a detail of the facade.

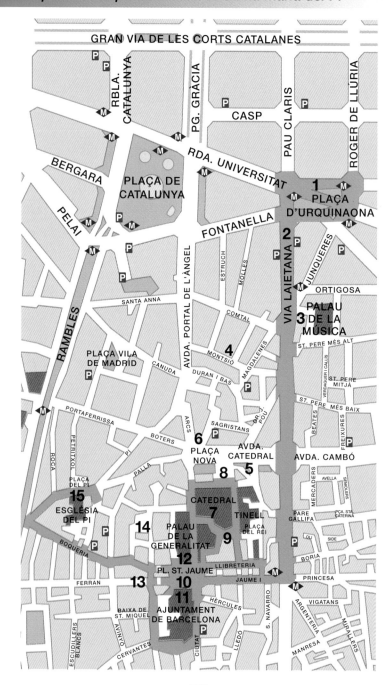

ITINERARY 2 (***) (A)

Visitors following this itinerary will be able to admire some of the city's oldest and most precious jewels, as we discover the original core of Barcino, as well as the Gothic Quarter, featuring the Cathedral. Here, in this section of the city, walled until the 19th century, were the Roman city and, subsequently, medieval Barcelona.

1.- Urquinaona Square (*) 2.- Via Laietana (*) 3.- Palau de la Música Catalana (***) 4.- Els Quatre Gats (**) 5.- Cathedral Avenue (*) 6.- Catalan Architects' College (*) 7.- Cathedral (***) 8.- Pla de la Catedral (**) 9.- Gothic Quarter (***) 10.- Sant Jaume Square (**) 11.- Generalitat Palace (***) 12.- City Hall (***) 13.- Ferran Street (*) 14.- Jewish quarter (**) 15.- Church of Santa Maria del Pi (***).

However, before we go back in time to the origins of Barcelona, we will pay a visit to several other places of interest close to the old centre. First is **Urquinaona Square (1)**, a square in the centre of town, from where we take **Via Laietana (2)** down towards the sea. This is the only street forming part of the Cerdà Plan which passes through the old part of the city. It was opened in 1907, designed to provide a fast thoroughfare between the sea and the centre, though it has to be admitted that its construction caused the destruction of a historically interesting area. The upper section of Via Laietana contains a number of interesting buildings, such as the 18th-century **Velers House**, former seat of the silkweavers' guild, recognizable by the murals decorating its walls, some salvaged from demolition, whilst others were newly constructed, worthy of note of is that of the banking entity "La Caixa" which also houses an exhibition hall.

Velers House.

"La Caixa" building.

If we turn off to the left as we descend Via Laietana, we come to the **Palau de la Música Catalana (3)** (Catalan

Concert House), a Modernist masterpiece built between 1905 and 1908 on the site of the Renaissance cloisters of the Convent dels Mínims. The "Palau" is the culminating work of the architect Domènech i Montaner. It was created as the seat and concert hall of the Orfeó Català, a choral society founded in 1891 by Lluís Millet and Amadeu Vives which played a fundamental role in popularising Catalan music. The Palau quickly became part of the cultural life of the city and became the natural venue for all expressions of national culture. Observing the exterior front of the building, it is impressive to see how it adapts to the labyrinth

Three views of the Palau de la Música Catalana.

Two details of the interior of the Palau de la Música Catalana.

of narrow streets in which it stands. The ceramic works adorning the front contrast with the reddish brick of the main construction, but its outstanding external feature is the enormous sculptural group on the corner of the first floor. This shows Saint George in full armour and in combat position, surrounded by figures from daily life at his feet is a damsel representing Catalan Music. This work, by Miquel Blay i Fàbregas, is considered a masterpiece of Catalan naturalist sculpture. Between two decorated columns on the main front of the building is a relief featuring the coat of arms of Catalonia on which are inscribed the words "Orfeó Català".

The building is divided into three sections: the entrances, the auditorium and the stage, united by numerous decorative elements which combine to create an atmosphere of harmony and unity. The entrance doors are formed by huge arches over which is a balcony which continues right round the building. Inside is Catalonia's most important concert hall, an oval area seating 2,000. The outstanding elements include the marble columns and floors, the immense staircases, the rich decoration throughout, the ceramic employed, the wide windows with multi-coloured glass and the large central skylight. In the centre of the stage is an impressive organ, whilst the whole is presided over by the coat of arms of Catalonia, a work by Lluís Bru. At either side project tremendous ceramic sculptures by Bru, Eusebi Arnau and others. An army of artists lent their skills to the construction and decoration of the "Palau", creating a monument of rich ornamentation and harmony. The Palau de la Música Catalana was given the Building of the Year Award in 1909 by the Town Council of Barcelona, and recently, in 1997, it was registered as part of the UNESCO World Heritage.

Still in Via Laietana, a little to the right is Montsió Street, whose number 3 is the first important work by the illustrious Catalan architect Puig i Cadafalch. Dating back to 1895, this is **Martí House**, better known as **Els Quatre Gats (4)**. The building features a garret and is crowned by a number of minarets, whilst the ground floor has pointed arches and a richly-sculptured gallery. Els Quatre Gats reached its moment of maximum splendour in the early part of the 20th century when it was a bar and cabaret whose illustrious customers included Santiago Rusiñol, Pere Romeo, Antoni Gaudí, etc. It later became the seat of the Cercle Artístic de Sant Lluc and is now a bar and restaurant.

The front of the bar-restaurant Els Quatre Gats.

A little further down, on the right, is Nova Square which, along with Pla de la Seu, to which it was joined in 1943, is the only element in the Cerdà Plan constructed horizontally in the old centre. This is **Cathedral Avenue (5)**, regularly the scene of concerts and other popular events, as well as a small daily market where second-hand books and antiques are sold. On Sunday mornings, lovers of Catalan popular culture gather here to dance the traditional sardana, and every Christmas the square forms the venue for a very special fair, the "Fira de Santa Llúcia", where all sorts of festive decoration and figures for cribs are sold.

Cathedral Avenue.

At one end of the wide avenue is the seat of the **Catalan Architects' College (6)**. The front of this building features engravings by Picasso representing scenes from popular fies-

Picasso mural in the Catalan Architects's College.

Main facade and interior of the Cathedral.

tas in Barcelona. The murals in the lobby are also by that great Spanish artist. The building, which contrasts deliberately with the surrounding architecture, was designed by Busquets.

Now, at last, we come to the **Cathedral (7)**, standing majestically in the same square. It is dedicated to the Holy Cross and Saint Eulàlia (former patron saint of Barcelona) and stands on the site of an earlier Romanesque cathedral which, it is thought, had in turn been constructed where a Paleo-Christian chapel dating back to the 4th century had formerly stood. Construction of the Gothic cathedral

began in 1298 with the Portal de Sant Iu and was completed in 1459. However, it must be added that the main front and the dome (featuring a slender spire) were not added until the late-19th century, designed by Josep Oriol Mestres and August Font.

Inside are a nave and two aisles of impressive height, with ambulatory and side chapels between the buttresses. Over these chapels is an upper gallery, giving the impression that there are two more aisles here, conferring greater light and space on the building. The main front has two octagonal belltowers supported

St. Eulalia crypt.

Christ of Lepanto.

by a transept. It is constructed in tyically Gothic style, as is reflected in its simple lines and sense of verticality. The sombre walls of the cathedral interior guard objects of enormous historical and artistic importance. Under the presbytery, which features a crucifix by the sculptor Frederic Marés (1976), is the **Crypt of Santa Eulàlia**. This has a curious vault, almost completely flat in shape and divided into two arches, under which is the tomb of the saint, which dates back to the 14th century and is supported by smooth alabaster columns. The **coro** features fine columns and a Mannerist floral frieze and is situated at the centre of the nave, occupying a large part of it. The stalls are by Pere Ca Anglada and Macià Bonafé (14th century) and feature fine painting and

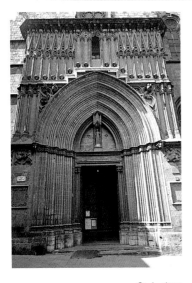

St. Iu door.

St. Eulalia door.

precious metalwork. Another important element in the Cathedral is the **Chapterhouse**, now the Chapel of the Santíssim, containing the statue of the *Sant Crist of Lepanto,* which accompanied John of Austria at the battle of Lepanto. Next to the **high altar** (consecrated in 1337) is a splen-

Mercy door.

Cloister.

Vault keystone "The Virgin of Compassion", in the main nave.

St. Llúcia chapel.

"Mercy" (Bartolomé Bermejo, 1490).

did wooden altarpiece dating back to the 15th century.

The cathedral is entered by various gates: the **Sant Iu door**, the oldest of these, which stands in Comtes Street, and those of **Santa Eulàlia**, **Santa Llúcia** and **Mercy door**. These gates also give access to the lovely 14th-century **cloister**, surrounded by chapels with large windows facing into the central courtyard, where are gardens and a Gothic fountain. These gardens are flanked on all sides by fine vaulted galleries with pointed arches. On Corpus Cristi it is traditional to place an empty eggshell on the upward-spouting waters of the fountain, so that it becomes a "dancing egg", rocked by the surging waters without falling. Adjoining the cloisters is the **Chapel of Santa Llúcia**, dating back to 1268. This chapel originally formed part of the Bishop's Palace, having been built by Bishop Arnau de Gurb. The cloister Chapterhouse contains the **Cathedral Museum**, with a small but valuable collection of religious works including Gothic and Renaissance paintings including the outstanding Mercy by Bartolomé Bermejo. Barcelona Cathedral was declared Historic-Artistic Monument of National Interest in 1929.

At the main entrance in **Pla de la Catedral (8)**, also known as Pla de la Seu, over the original Mons Taber, we see on our left the **Deacon's House** and, on the right, the **Pia Almoina House**, a 14th-century edifice which was destroyed in 1400 and rebuilt 23 years later to house the charitable institution of the same name, founded in the 11th century. At present the Pia Almoina House is

Frederic Marès' Museum.

Augustus Roman temple.

the headquarters of the **Diocese Museum** which puts on exhibitions of religious art that embraces from the romanic period to the present day.

The entire zone around the cathedral is known as the **Gothic Quarter (9)**. This district is made up of a veritable labyrinth of narrow streets which conserve a historic air and are full of fascinating details, interesting shops and beautiful palaces to delight the strolling visitor. This is one of the most characteristic and historically important areas of the entire city.

Turning right outside the cathedral, taking Comtes Street (adjoining the Pia Almoina House), we come to Sant Iu Square . At number 5 of this square is the **Frederic Marés' Museum**, containing works donated by the artist himself and occupying part of the Palau Reial Major. Inside, the building is divided into one section containing sculptures and another, entitled "Sentimental", illustrating crafts and daily life from the 15th to the 19th century.

Near to here in Calle Paradís, a millstone incrusted in the roadway tell us the highest point of Mons Taber, 12 metres in altitude, a hill that raised up just in the centre of the ancient roman Barcino. But the most interesting can be found in the inner patio of the gothic house opposite this millstone. For some years this has been the headquarters of the Excursionist Centre of Catalonia. These are the remains of a **roman temple dedicated to Augustus** of which four

Plaça del Rei.

large columns of the Corinthian order and part of the wooden planking that covers the temple are still preserved. A little further on, we come to the **Clariana Padellàs House** (Veguer Street, 4), containing the **City History Museum**, transferred here from its orginal seat in Mercaders Street in the mid-20th century, though the building dates back to the late-15th. During excavation work preparatory to rebuilding the foundations, remains of the Roman settlement were discovered, and it was decided to preserve them by transferring the City History Museum here. The museum collections include architectural elements, documents, maps, models, thermal baths, remains from a Visigoth necropolis and Moorish baths. The excavated ruins go right up the original basilica and baptistery in the very the cathedral foundations. The site was declared Historic-Artistic Monument of National Interest in 1962.

Next, we come to the **Plaça del Rei**, square one of the most interesting squares in the city, for centuries the site of the straw and forage market. This is a medieval site containing the Palau del Lloctinent, the Palau Reial Major and the Chapel of Santa Agueda. Its name ("Square of the King") derives from the illustrious nature of these buildings flanking it, but in fact this was originally a palace courtyard. Its present arrangement is due to King Martin, the Humane, who wished by enclosing it to preserve the space from the bustle and noise of the nearby streets. Before the construction of the Palau del Lloctinent, which took up much of the available space, there were trees and a Neo-Gothic fountain here, though the excavations carried out this century obliged the entire square to be remodelled, giving it its present aspect. Entering the square, we can admire a sculpture by Chillida and, on the left, the **Palau del Lloctinent** (Royal Lieutenant's Palace), constructed when the court was transferred from Barcelona and the palace divided between the Inquisition, the Royal Audience and the Mayor's Office so as to provide suitable apartments for the lieutenant of the city and for the sessions of the Audience. The palace was designed by Antoni Carbonell in the 15th century as a single Renaissance-style block. The building was later remodelled and since 1836 has housed the Archivo de la Corona de Aragó, one of the most important medieval archives in the world. In 1994 it was moved to its new head-quarters in the town of Sant Cugat del Vallès.

In the angle joining the buildings Palau del Llochtinent and the Palau Reial Major the **Torre del rei Martí** raises up. This is a five-storey watchtower built in 1555 whose purpose was to watch the coast to prevent surprise attacks. The visiting and climbing the tower is included in the route offered by the city's History Museum. This route also passes by Palau Reial Maior and the Santa Agata Chapel and comes up to the foot of the Cathedral so you can admire the remains of the primitive episcopal building of

Royal Lieutenant's Palace.

Tinell Room.

Santa Àgueda Chapel.

Monument to Ramon Berenguer "The Great".

Barcelona, repaired in the visigothic period.

The **Palau Reial Major**, the oldest building in the square, was the residence of counts of Barcelona and monarchs of Catalonia-Aragon. The original building dates back to the 11th century, though it has since been much modified. In the 12th century, Ramón Berenguer IV ordered the construction of a new building opposite Comtes Street, later to house the courts of the Inquisition. Later, in the 13th century, Jaume I further extended the palace, and reforms were also carried out under the reigns of Jaume II and Alfons, the Benign (14th century). However, the most important transformation of the building was carried out under Pere, the Ceremonious, also in the 14th century. Alterations at this time included the creation of the **Saló del Tinell**, a huge rectangular chamber ribbed by six semicircular arches which are joined at the ends by vaults supporting the central wooden ceiling. The room was designed by Guillem Carbonell and decorated by Jaume Desfeu. It witnessed such important historic events as the reception before the Catholic Monarchs of the triumphant Christopher Columbus, returning from America in 1493, and also served as the chapel of rest for the remains of Charles of Vienna and John II, when, as a sign of respect, the knights of the cortège were allowed to enter the building on their horses.

On the right, adjacent to Ramon Berenguer III Square, is the **Chapel of Santa Agueda**, built over the old Roman walls in the 14th century, commissioned by Jaume II to replace the old oratory of the Palace. The Gothic chapel has a single nave with four sections, and features a polychrome wood ceiling. The apse is adorned with the coats of arms of Catalonia and Aragon. The altarpiece is an outstanding work of Catalan Gothic art known as the retable del Condestable, by Jaume Huguet (1465). It replaced another work, now lost, by Ferrer Bassa.

Leaving the square, on the corner with Via Laietana, is the bronze equestrian **statue of Ramon Berenguer the Great**, by Josep Llimona. In the same Ramon Berenguer el Gran Sqaure we can also see some remains of the Roman walls, which here reach a height of seven metres. There are also three two-storey towers with semicircular arches in this square.

Ardiaca House.

Retracing our steps back towards the Cathedral, this time turning to the left, opposite the Chapel of Santa Llúcia is the **Ardiaca House**, forming a single block with the Deacon House. This began to be built in the 12th century in Catalan Gothic Flamboyant style over part of the old Roman walls. Alterations were carried out by Archdeacon Lluís Desplà around the turn of the 16th century, and further modifications were almost continual right up to the present century. The entrance doorway has a Roman design with Renaissance ornamentation, and gives onto a central courtyard. Next to the Renaissance gateway is a marble letterbox by Lluís Domènech i Montaner, featuring swallows and a tortoise, "symbols of the speed with which we would like our messages to arrive and the slowness with which they seem to be delivered into our hands". Over the years the Casa de

Modernist letterbox on the facade of the Ardiaca House.

Episcopal Palace.

St Phillip Neri Church.

Detail of a house in the square, St. Phillip Neri.

l'Ardiaca has served successively as the seat of the Barcelona college of advocates, the city archives and, most recently, the Municipal Institute of History.

The original **Episcopal Palace** was built in the 13th century, though all that remains of it are a few elements conserved in the courtyard and the Romanesque galleries. The rest dates back to the alterations made in the 17th century, including the splendid throne room, decorated with scenes from the Old Testament.

Taking Bisbe Street then Sant Sever Street, we come to the Saint Phillip Neri Church, which stands in the square of the same name (at 9, Sant Sever Street is the **Sant Sever Church**, which has an interesting interior, as well as featuring a statue of the saint on the front). Sant Felip Neri Square stands on the site of the former Cemetery of Montjuïc el Bisbe. Badly damaged during the Spanish Civil War, the church was later remodelled, though the shellmarks on its walls were kept as a reminder of that tragic episode. In the centre of the square is a fountain with two graceful acacias, whilst it is flanked by the **Boilermakers' Guild building** (transferred here stone by stone) and the seat of the **Shoemakers' Guild**, which now houses the **Antique Footwear Muse-**

um, with a collection of antique shoes and footwear belonging to famous personages. **Saint Phillip Neri Church** and the adjacent monastery formerly belonged to the 17th-century Order of the Congregation of Lay Clergy of the Oratory. It is built in Baroque style and has a single nave with inter-communicated chapels. Inside are various Baroque and Neo-Classical altars. The simple lines of its front are crowned with a niche containing a statue of the Virgin. The adjoining monastery contains a closed two-storey cloister.

On the same Bisbe Street is the **Canonges House,** joined to the Generalitat Palace by a bridge and, despite its Gothic style, built in 1928. It comprises a group of buildings

Bisbe Street.

Main facade of the City Hall building.

Saló de Cent. City Hall.

dating from the 14th century that have undergone a great deal of restoration and were formerly used as the residences for the presidents of the Generalitat (Catalan Autonomous Government).

Finally, we come to **Sant Jaume Square (10)**, an extension to the old Roman Agora and former site of the Sant Jaume Church. This has always been the seat of political power, and now serves also as the venue for various events, particularly celebrations of famous sporting victories and demonstrations. The square did not begin to take its present shape until 1823, when Jaume I Street (leading here from Via Laietana) and Ferran Street (leading to the Ramblas) were opened. The square contains, opposite one another, the Generalitat Palace (seat of the autonomous government, whose origins go back to the 13th-century Corts Catalanes) and the Ajuntament, or City Hall.

Barcelona City Hall (11) consists, in fact, of three communicating buildings (the "old", the "new" and the "super-new" buildings). This explains the profusion of styles to be seen in it. The "old" part was constructed by Pere Llobet in the 14th century, when the Saló de Cent came into being (there is a plaque bearing the inscription "1373"), extending an old house purchased from the Consell de Cent. In 1399, Arnau Bargués designed the Gothic main front giving onto what is now Ciutat Street, with a statue of Archangel Raphael, still to be seen here. After fire destroyed the Sant Jaume Church in 1822, moreover, the

Gothic front of Barcelona's City Hall.

city hall was extended, with the creation of the present Sant Jaume Square. The extension, designed by Josep Mas i Vila, has a Neo-Classical front. The entrance features statues of King Jaume I (left) and Conseller Joan Fiveller (defender of municipal rights). Later, in 1933, the "new" building came into being, consisting of an office block giving onto Ciutat Street. Another building, the "supernew" section in Sant Miquel Square, was added in 1958.

Entering the building by the present main front, we see a Gothic central courtyard from which rise two staircases, the "black staircase", so-named due to the colour of the marble of which it is constructed, and the "staircase of honour". The building contains various splended rooms, among them the **Saló de Cent** which, though much-altered, contains interesting finely-upholstered benches and decoration reminding us of its Gothic origins, with constant references to the medieval city guilds. From the wooden ceiling hang magnificent lamps decorated with motifs of the Kingdom of Catalonia-Aragon. The **Saló de Sessions** served as the residence of Queen Maria Christina of the House of Hapsburg when she attended in 1888 Universal Exhibition in company of the future King Alfonso XIII. The panelled floor features the coat of arms of the city. The **Saló de Cròniques** was for years the scene of important receptions,

St. Just square (very close to the Sant Jaume's square): St. Just and Shepherd Church and gothic fountain.

Generalitat Palace.

and is hung with magnificent sepia-coloured paintings depicting famous historic events.

Opposite the City Hall is the **Generalitat Palace (12)**. In 1403 it was decided that, due to the increasing activities of the Corts Catalanes, that it was essential to find a seat from which to direct all its administrative actions. The original building gave onto Sant Honorat Street, in the Jewish quarter. Towards the 14th century, the building was extended to Sant Sever Street and the current front, giving onto Sant Jaume Square, a Renaissance work by Pere Blay. The palace was originally built as a large chapel dedicated to Saint James, which can be seen at the entrance. Inside is a Gothic **courtyard** with an open staircase leading to the first floor, also open, with arches supported by slender columns. The **Saló de Sant Jordi** dates back to the 15th century and features a star-decorated vault in whose centre is Saint George surrounded by angels. The **Pati dels Tarongers** ("Courtyard of the Orange Trees"), by Pau Mateu and Tomàs Barsa has a fountain crowned by a statuette of the patron saint of the city, by Frederic Galcerà (1926), as well as busts of Prat de la Riba and Francesc Macià. From here, we can see the belltower, whose medieval bells still ring out. In recent years, various pieces have been returned to their original sites, such as the bust of Macià, whilst new works include the decoration of a room by the painter Jordi Alumà, the stone and bronze reliefs by Josep Maria

Generalitat Palace: Orange Tree Patio and gothic gallery.

Ferran Street.

Subirachs, the large panel dedicated to the "Four Gospels", by Antoni Tàpies, and a painting of Saint George by Montserrat Gudiol, in her characteristic red tones.

Leaving Sant Jaume Square, we now take **Ferran Street (13)**, which leads us back to the Ramblas. All around now is the old **Jewish quarter (14)**, the largest of medieval Catalonia. Just a few traces of that period can still be glimpsed in Sant Domènech Street and in Marlet Street, where there is a funeral stone dating back to the year 1314. The area contains many interesting streets, such as **La Palla**, containing interesting book and antique shops, or **Petritxol**, lined by 16th-18th-century buildings, as well as Barcelona's oldest art gallery, the **Sala Parés** (1884). Visitors should also drop in to one of the many milk bars in Petritxol Street and try the excellent hot chocolate with cream and melindros.

La Palla Street and Banys Nous Street both lead us to the last sight on our itinerary. The **Church of Santa Maria del Pi (15)** stands in the square of the same name. Construction began in 1332 in Catalan Gothic style. The church consists of a single nave and is practically bare of all sculptural adornment. The octagonal belltower is 54 metres high. Inside, the 18th-century altars of Sant Miquel and La Verge dels Desemparats, both by Ramón Amadeu are interesting, as is the glass decoration of the west portal, by Antoni Viladomat. A lateral front opens onto Sant Josep Oriol Square, whilst the main front looks over the Pi Square and features a lovely 12-sided rose window, thought to be the largest in the world. **Pi Square** ("Pine") is so-named as the square was built around such a tree. The site is mentioned in the 10th century as the centre of a new section of the city outside the walls. Nowadays, at weekends, the square is taken over by painters who exhibit and sell their works.

Church of Santa Maria del Pi.

Petritxol Street.

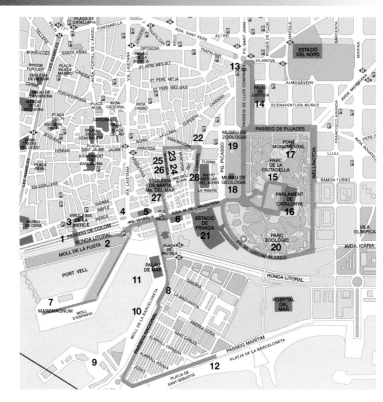

ITINERARY 3 (***) (M and A)

We begin this itinerary from the maritime frontage of Barcelona, at the point closest to the old quarter, continue through the old seafaring district of Barceloneta, which brings us to Ciutadella Park, and finish up in the Born district, with interesting sites such as the Picasso Museum and a jewel of Catalan Gothic architecture, the Church of Santa Maria del Mar.

1.- Passeig de Colom (*). 2.- Moll de la Fusta (*). 3.- La Mercè Basilica (***). 4.- Post Office Building (**). 5.- The Llotja (Exchange) (**). 6.- Porxos d'en Xifré (**). 7.- Maremàgnum (**). 8.- Barceloneta district (**). 9.- Port Vell (*). 10.- Port Vell Marina (*). 11.- Moll Nou (*). 12.- Beaches of Barceloneta (**). 13.- Arch of Triumph (***). 14.- Justice Palace (**). 15.- Ciutadella Park (**). 16.- Catalan Parliament (*). 17.- Ciutadella Park Cascade (**). 18.- Geology Museum (*). 19.- Zoological Museum (*). 20.- Zoo (***). 21.- France train station (**). 22.- Chocolate Museum (**). 23.- Montcada Street (***). 24.- Picasso Museum (***). 25.- Textile and Costume Museum (***). 26.- Barbier-Mueller Museum of Precolumbian Art (**). 27.- Church of Santa Maria del Mar (***). 28.- Passeig del Born an Born Market (*).

Passeig de Colom and the Moll de la Fusta.

Our route begins at the Monument to Columbus (see Itinerary I), from where we take **Passeig de Colom (1)**, whose surroundings were recently transformed into a seaward-facing leisure area in the first development in the process of recovering the sea for the city. This is the Moll de Bosch i Alsina dock, popularly known as the **Moll de la Fusta (2),** where once stood the seawall, built in the 16th century and finally demolished in 1881. The dock was originally used to store wood, but the activities of the port and increasing traffic made it impossible to use this space. Plans were therefore drawn up to convert it into an area for leisure and relaxation, whilst the stretch inland was converted into a fast thoroughfare for

"Face of Barcelona" sculpture, in the Moll de la Fusta.

La Mercè basilica.

Statue of the Virgin of Mercy.

cars and lorries. The alterations, directed by Solà Morales, were completed in 1987. The quayside today is made up of two platforms: the lower is a pedestrian walkway, and the upper level acts as a kind of balcony over the port.

At the end of this promenade, opposite the sea, is the **La Mercè Basilica (3)**, standing in the square of the same name. In around 1835, this church formed part of a Mercedarian convent, and it now contains the statue of the patron saint of Barcelona, Our Lady of Mercy. This is a lovely Gothic carving, dressed in golden robes, by Pere Moragues (c. 1361). The church consists of a single nave with eight side chapels and an open transept

Post Office building.

crowned by a dome. The building is sumptuously decorated in Late-Baroque style, with marble and stucco adornments. The statue of La Mercè venerated in the church is a copy of the original, which was destroyed during the Spanish Civil War. Great sporting triumphs are celebrated here, the victorious team offering its trophy to the Virgin.

From Mercè Square, we take Mercè Street to Antonio López Square, offering splendid views of the **Post Office Building (4)**. Built in 1927, this is a monumental three-storey edifice, two of whose floors are communicated via a huge central space illuminated by a glass dome. The front, with its Classical air, features tow towers, one at either end, though the one giving on to Via Laietana is higher in order to emphasise the importance of this thoroughfare, linking the port with the Eixample district. The exterior of the building is adorned with allegorical and ornamental sculptures.

Nearby is the Pla del Palau, in which stands the **Llotja (Exchange) (5)**, used in medieval times as a store for goods and a centre for commercial transaction. In 1380, King Pere III, the Ceremonious, commissioned the construction of the original building, destroyed during the War of Spanish Succession, after which it remained out of service until 1771, they year which the Junta de Comercio recovered it for its own use. Between 1915 and 1994 it housed the Borsa de Barcelona (Barcelona Stock Exchange) and at present it is the headquarters of the Sant Jordi Fine Arts Academy. The building has a rectangular ground-plan with three large aisles separated by rows of round arches supporting a polychrome wood ceiling. The Neo-Classical front features an arcade made up of Tuscan columns. The inner staircase is adorned with allegorical marble figures exalting industry and trade. The site was declared a Historic-Artistic Monument of National Interest in 1931.

This same area contains, on one corner of the Pla del Palau, opposite the Passeig d'Isabel II, the **Porxos d'en Xifré (6)**. This is a row of houses whose base is made up of a series of 21 arches forming an arcade harmoniously supporting a row of 3-storey buildings with balconied windows. The ornamentation takes the form of a number of busts of personages linked to the discovery of America and motifs referring to overseas trade. The site is named after Josep Xifré i Casas, a famous Catalan trader who emigrated to America to seek his fortune. On his return, he purchased the site opposite the Llotja where, in the mid-19th-century, Josep Boixereu and Francesc Vila built this block of houses, unusual for their times, one of which Xifré reserved for himself. Under El Porxos is the famous **Les Set Portes** restaurant, which serves traditional Catalan specialities.

From here, or by the Pasarela de Mar, opposite the monument dedicated to Columbus, you can gain access to **Maremàgnum (7)** which is a large leisure centre that since its inauguration in the mid 1990s has become one of the favourite spots of the people of Barcelona

Porxos d'en Xifré.

Maremàgnum.

as well as those who visit the city. It covers a ground area of 55 hectares and embraces of a large number of restaurants, bars, terraces, amusement arcades and various shops in addition to eight cinema screens. The **Barcelona Aquarium** is also located in the Maremàgnum, the largest and most important aquarium in the world based on Mediterranean marine life (the stroll along 80 metres of transparent tunnel below an immense oceanic circular aquarium and the fixed expressions of more than 300 different species, including sharks, is unforgettable). Then there is **IMAX**, a cinema that combines three large format projection systems: the Imax with a flat screen measuring seven stories high, the Omnimax with a

Barcelona Aquarium.

900 m² dome and 3D or three dimensional projection.

Following the sea front, we come to the popular **Barceloneta district (8)**, a typical fishing quarter completely impregnated by the salt smell of the sea. Its origins go back to army provisions to house the population displaced in the 18th century by plans to construct the Ciutadella. The streets of the district were laid out in grid-like fashion, easy to control. Barceloneta was heavily bombed during the Civil War and the streets which now exist were built on the sites of houses destroyed at that time. The district now contains hundreds of typical fish restaurants.

The Old Dock, or **Port Vell (9)**, forms a vital part of this district. Recent alterations have radically transformed its landscape, the docks and jetties converted into a new complex offering a variety of facilities. An example is the renovation of the old Magatzems Generals del Comerç, a series of warehouses built from 1880-90 to serve the docks. These have now been converted into the **Palau de Mar**, a building measuring 30,000 m², that house offices, the **History Museum of Catalonia** and a number of restaurants.

IMAX cinema.

Palau de Mar.

Port Vell Marina.

Next to it is the Moll de la Barceloneta, along which dock is situated the **Port Vell Marina (10)**, which includes the old commercial and industrial boatyards. The entire zone was rehabilitated and furnished with complete services for sports craft. The new pleasure harbour has capacity for over 400 boats: yachts are moored at the Moll dels Pescadors, whilst boats up to 25 metres in length can be accommodated in the Dipòsits and Barceloneta docks. The harbour developers also planned a ser-

St. Sebastian's Tower and Clock Tower .

vice area at the **Moll Nou (11)**, created by joining two former boat-repair jetties. This service area is presided over by the **Saint Sebastian's Tower** and the old Vulcano boatyards. Here also is the largest dry dock in the Mediterranean, 12,000 square metres equipped with the latest technology. This new service area and marina has made the Port of Barcelona one of the largest complexes of its type and an important stop on Mediterranean sea routes. In the area, also, is the **Clock Tower** (1772), which used to signal when ships left the port and to serve as a lighthouse.

Up to 1981, there were only six hectares of beach in the Barceloneta district. The entire eastern coastline was closed off by factories, railway lines and rubble. Barcelona's

beaches, those of **Sant Sebastià and Barceloneta (12)**, and those north of the marina were regenerated through the construction of six jetties and the installation of leisure and sports facilities. There are now 18 hectares of beaches, stretching five kilometres from Barceloneta to the River Besòs.

From Barceloneta, we enter Ciutadella Park by the entrance on **Passeig de Lluís Companys**, from which point rises the **Arc de Triomf (13)**. This triumphal arch was built by Josep Vilaseca i Casanovas in 1888 to serve as the entrance to the Universal Exhibition of the same year. The monument is built in bare brick, glazed ceramic, stone and iron features a frieze at the top, whilst its form reflects the tendency of the time to recover the Mudéjar and Mozarab styles. Its reliefs are decorated with friezes celebrating industry, trade, agriculture, art and science. Each main front is crowned by the royal coat of arms with, below, that of Barcelona presiding over the emblems of the Spanish provinces.

Another artistic jewel adorning the Passeig de Lluís Companys is the **Justice Palace (14)**, left to Arch of Triumph, built between 1887 and 1907. Although constructed during the Modernist period, its architects, Josep Domènech and Enric Sagnier, employed an eclectic style in its design. The palace is made up of two rectangular sections, each with two courtyards. These two buildings are separated by a cen-

tral body containing the entrances and the high court. At the corners are eight spectacular towers crowned by cupolas decorated with the coats of arms of the other Catalan provinces. Inside, there is a fine marble staircase leading up to the splended chamber known as that of the *passos perduts* ("lost steps"). At the end of Passeig de Lluís Companys can be made out the **Ciutadella Park (15)**, the second largest park in Barcelona. It began to be built in 1871, on the site formerly occupied by Philip V's troops and which had also been used as a prison. This citadel was demolished and architect Josep Fontseré commissioned to design the park. The 1888 Universal Exhibition was held here. The

Arch of Triumph.

65

Aerial view Ciutadella Park.

Cascade in Ciutadella Park.

Ciutadella is made up of a series of paths and gardens arranged around the central Armes Square. This square contains an oval pond presided over by **"Desconsol"** **(Grief)**, the most famous of the works of the sculptor Josep Llimona. Opposite this is the **Catalan Parliament (16)**. The park also contains a lake, near to which is a wide esplanade with a bandstand mental **fountain**

(17) designed by Fontseré and Gaudí. The park also contains various important natural science museums, including the **Geological Museum (18)**, also known as the Martorell Museum and the oldest in Barcelona, and the **Zoological Museum (19)**, housed in the former Exhibition café-restaurant, designed by Domènech i Montaner. Other buildings worth noting in the park are: the **Umbracle** (the work of Josep Fontseré i Mestres, made of iron and wood constructed between 1883 and 1885), the **Hivernacle** (designed by Josep Amargós and built between 1883 and 1887), both of which have been recently restored.

Finally, **Barcelona Zoo (20)**, founded here in 1894, is one of the finest in Europe. The big star of the zoo was the albino gorilla Floquet de Neu (Snowflake), the only primate

"Grief", work of the artists Josep Llimona, 1903, and the Parliament of Catalonia.

of its kind ever found on the planet; it came to the zoo in 1966 barely three years old and died the 24th of November 2003.

Leaving the park, we take Avenue Marquès de l'Argentera until we reach another railway station, the **France rail station (21)**. This edi-

Zoological Museum and the Hivernacle (Greenhouse).

"The Umbrella Lady", in the gardens in Ciutadella Park.

The albino gorilla "Snowflake".

fice was completed in 1930 on the site of another railway station which had become too small to handle the growing rail traffic of Barcelona. The building consists of two huge metallic arches forming 30-metre high naves and a huge Classicist-style vestibule. In its day, it was one of the largest in Europe. The decoration of the vestibule, by Raimon Duran and Salvador Soteras, won the city council prize in 1930.

From here, we enter the labyrinth of the **Ribera district**, more specifically the district known as **Born**. First we take Comerç Street as far as Princesa Street. Those who have a sweet tooth must not miss the chance to visit number 36 Comerç Street the **Chocolate Museum (22)**, wholly dedicated to this product since its arrival in Europe and an excellent opportunity to see the typical and imaginative *mones* de Pascua

France rail station.

(chocolate sculptures for Easter) produced in Catalonia.

We continue along **Princesa Street** as far as **Montcada Street(23)**. The origins of this charming narrow street go back to the 12th century, when the ruling classes decided to connect the old centre to the new coastal district of the city. During the 14th-18th centuries, Montcada Street was the residence of the Barcelonan aristocracy, and fine palaces were built all along it. As a result, the street is now a living monument to Catalan medieval civil architecture, unequalled anywhere else in the city for interest and quality. The **Picasso Museum (24)**, a much visited treasure trove of work, is housed in the old palaces of Berenguer d'Aguilar (15th century) and the Baró de Castellet y de Meca, and has recently been enlarged with the palace-houses Mauri and Finestres. The Picasso Museum was

Montcada Street.

opened in 1963, its collection based on a donation by Jaume Sabater, a close friend of the painter, and contributions from Picasso himself, as well as members of artist's family. There are important collections of Picasso's paintings, ceramics and engravings here. The major

"The Meninas of Velázquez", by Pablo R. Picasso. Picasso Museum.

Entrance to the Picasso Museum.

paintings exhibited include "Science and Charity", *Els Desamparats* ("Mother and Child") and the series of 44 interpretations of Velazquez's **Las Meninas**.

Montcada Street also contains other palace-houses such as the **Custòdia house** (at number 1) dating from the 18th century that looks out on to the Plaçoleta de Marcús, next to the **Marcús Chapel**. It is romanic and the only vestige of a charitable complex founded in the 12th century. Then there is the **Marquesos de Lió house** (at number 16) dating from the 14th century which today is the headquarters of the **Textile and Costume Museum (25)** which contains an important collection of garments from the 4th to the 20th century. The **Nadal house** (at number 14) today houses the **Barbier-Mueller Museum of Precolumbian Art (26)**. The **Dalmases House** (number 20), dating from the 15th century, houses the **Òmnium**

Cultural association with fine reliefs on the staircases of the central courtyard. Then there is the **Cervelló-Guidice house** (at number 25) dating from the 15th century which houses the **Maeght Gallery**.

At the end of the street is Santa Maria Square, dominated by the **Church of Santa Maria del Mar (27),** the finest of Catalan Gothic churches, built between 1329 and 1384, during the reign of Alfonso IV, the Benign. The original architects were Berenguer de Montagut and Ramon Despuig. The church was begun during a period of famous Catalan conquests overseas and became a symbol of the power of the new merchant classes, and became known as the "Cathedral of the Sea". The building consists of a huge nave and two aisles, sep-arated by slender octagonal columns. The nave is divided into four square sections and the aisles into half-squares. The buttresses of the side walls contain tiny chapels, three for each section. On a second level,

Marcús Chapel.

Dalmases' Palace patio.

Facade and interior (following page) of Santa Maria del Mar.

up to the height of the nave, the buttresses can be seen in the exterior. The apse has an ambulatory with several radial chapels.

The main front is flanked by two octagonal towers and features an imposing central doorway. The tympanum contains a statue of the Saviour between the Virgin and Saint John. This front dates back to the first half of the 14th century, though in 1428 an earthquake destroyed the original rose window, which was replaced in the 15th century by a large, Gothic Flamboyant one. The two-storey octagonal towers were completed in 1496 (west tower) and 1902 (east tower). The presbytery over the crypt was constructed after the Civil War. In 1931 Santa Maria del Mar was designated a Historic-Artistic Monument of National Interest.

Opposite the main front of the Church of Santa Maria del Mar, we find the animated **Born Esplanade** and the old **Born Market (28)**, an interesting iron construction built in 1874 in accordance with a project by Josep Fontseré i Mestres. It operated as a market until 1971, since when, it has been used for diverse cultural activities. More recently, construction works to house a library have revealed important Roman Ruins beneath the foundations. The district of Born is an area filled with shops, art galleries, bars and restaurants and is especially popular by night.

Passeig del Born and old Born Market.

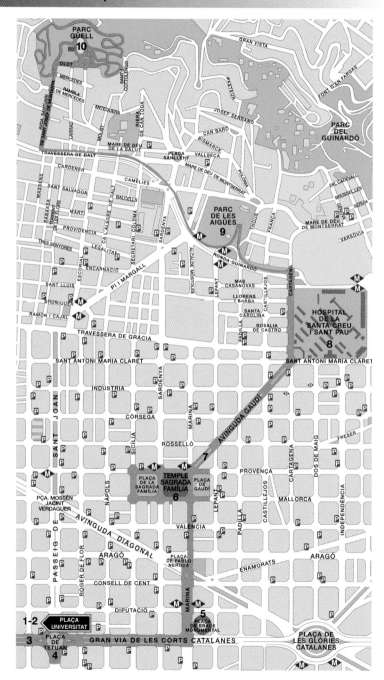

ITINERARY 4 (**) (M and A)

We begin our fourth itinerary in Universitat Square, close to Catalunya Square, reached by Ronda de la Universitat and the central Bergara Street and Pelai Street. Our steps will take us from the city centre to one of the hills at its limits, on the way allowing us to contemplate some of the finest jewels of Catalan Modernism.

1.- Universitat Square (*) 2.- University (**) 3.- Gran Via de les Corts Catalanes (*) 4.- Tetuan Square (*) 5.- La Monumental Bullring (**) 6.- Sagrada Familia (***) 7.- Gaudí Avenue (*) 8.- Hospital de la Santa Creu i Sant Pau (***) 9.- Les Aigües park and tower (**) 10.- Park Güell (**)

The name of **Universitat Square (1)**, where we begin this itinerary, is due to the fact that the square is presided over by the Central University building or **University (2)**, which dates back to the year 1868. The designer, Elies Rogent, took his inspiration from the Catalan Romanesque style when planning the building, which is 136 metres in length and 83 in width. The front contains a central body, higher than the rest of the building, and two square towers at either end, one of which with clock and belfry. Inside are fine two-storey cloisters, identical in structure. The main staircase leads from the vestibule to the rectorate, the central hall (outstanding by virtue of its Neo-Mudéjar decoration), the chapel, the aula magna and the library, which contains over 200,000 volumes as

Universitat Square and the University of Barcelona building.

Modernist houses in Gran Via: Golferichs House (Gran Via/Viladomat) and the old Lactancia House (Gran Via/Calàbria).

Coliseum cinema, on the Gran Via close to the Rambla de Catalunya.

well as medieval and Renaissance documents.

In 1717, Philip V ordered Barcelona's university closed as a punishment for the Catalan people's failure to support him during the War of Succession. From then on, the only centre of higher studies in Catalonia was in Cervera. In 1845, the University of Barcelona was created once more, and was, for the moment, the only one in the Principality. The building was declared an Artistic-Historic Monument of National Interest in 1970.

Behind the university building is the **Seminar Conciliar**, also by Elies Rogent, dating from 1887, which today is the headquarters of the Faculty of Theology of Catalonia and the Catholic Institutc of Social Studies of Barcelona (ICESB).

We now take **Gran Via de les Corts Catalanes (3)**, a wide avenue which crosses the city from south-west to north-east and is one of the longest thoroughfares in Barcelona. Between Passeig de Gràcia and Rambla de Catalunya, there is a gardened section. The Comèdia Cinema, formerly **Marcet Palace**, is an interesting example of the little palaces lining the promenade and which at first served as the residences of the very Modernist architects who built them. Still on Gran Via, going northwards, we come to **Tetuan Square (4)**, in the centre of which is the **Monument to Doctor Robert** (1842-1902), illustrious doctor and founder of the Hospital of Sant Pau, mayor of the city and president of the Regionalist League. The monument is a good example of Catalan Modernist sculpture and is erected over a stone fountain of undulating lines. The piece,

Hotel Ritz, on the corner of Gran Via and Roger de Llúria.

Tetuan Square.

La Monumental Bullring.

in marble and bronze, features eight allegorical figures representing the different activities of the doctor, whilst at the rear there is a group of figures carved in stone representing a scene at a doctor's surgery. The square was recently completely remodelled, with the construction of a stone platform raising the fountain's surroundings by one metre above the average height of the square, improving the view of the monument. A sculptured fountain, by Frederic Marès, standing in the gardens around it renders homage to the local traditional dance, the Sardana.

As we continue in the same directio, at the crossroads of Gran Via with Marina Street we come to the **La Monumental Bullring (5)**. This is the only Modernist bullring in the world,

and the only one of the two in Barcelona where the fiesta nacional still takes place. Designed by Ignasi Mas i Morell and Domènech Sugranyes, it features oval-domed towers covered with blue and white ceramics forming arabesques. **The Bullfighting Museum** inside displays stuffed bulls, posters and a collection of colourful bullfighters' costumes.

We now leave Gran Via to take Marina Street where, on the left, we are soon confronted by the imposing **Sagrada Familia (6)**, one of the city's most representative and emblematic monuments, as well as one of the most popular with visitors. Gaudí began to direct work on this cathedral in 1883, following the original plans drawn up by Francesc De Paula

Sagrada Familia: Birth facade.

Antoni Gaudí i Cornet (1852-1926) is considered to be the ultimate and most original proponent of Catalan modernism. His most famous work is without doubt the Sagrada Familia Temple. He joined this project in 1883 and devoted himself exclusively to it from 1914 onwards until his death in 1926. However, Barcelona also has other buildings designed by this genius: Vicens House (1878-1885), the Güell Pavilions (1884-1887), Güell Palace (1885-1890), St. Teresa College (1888-1889), Calvet House (1898-1900), Figueras House or Bellesguard (1900-1902), Güell Park (1900-1914), Batlló House (1904-1906), Milà House "La Pedrera" (1905-1910), not to mention a number of minor works such as the street lamps in the Royal Square.

Relief by Josep Llimona, Sagrada Familia on the crypt altar.

Villar. The construction of the church began with the initiative of the "Associació Espiritual de Devots de Sant Josep", founded by Josep Maria Bocabella, the main impulsor of the idea of dedicating a church to the exaltation of Saint Joseph and the Holy Family as symbols of stability and family values. Its construction has always been totally reliant upon donations.

Gaudí conceived of the Sagrada Familia as the great modern church Barcelona needed, designing a complex system of Christian symbols and extending the original dimensions to make a church with a nave and four aisles with transept and apse and an exterior ambulatory. He also envisaged 18 large parabolic towers symbolising the 12 Apostles, the four Evangelists, the Virgin Mary and Jesus Christ, this last planned to stand out over all the others at a height of 170 metres. Gaudí's first measure was to

Apse steeples.

The first work undertaken by Gaudí when he joined the Sagrada Familia building project was to finish off the crypt begun by Villar.

The Birth facade: the central portal or Chasity portal.

complete the crypt begun by Villar. Later from 1883 to 1884, he constructed the apse, using realistic ornamentation. He had planned to build three fronts, each formed by groups of four towers dedicated to the twelve Apostles. However, due to the architect's premature death, run down by a tram, in 1926, he was only able to complete the first, the "Front of the Birth", which gives onto Marina Street, opposite Gaudí Avenue. The other façades planned were those of the Passion and the Death to the west

View of the parish schools with the bell towers in the background.

Facade of the Passion.

and that of the Glory in the south (now impossible to complete due to lack of space). Between the towers are three doorways, dedicated to Faith, Hope (adorned with the anagram of Mary) and Charity, with different sculptural scenes. The towers, crowned with colourful mosaics, are over 100 metres in height. The **parish schools** in the south-east corner of the site are decorated with representations of scenes from the Parables. The belltowers or spires, slightly convex in form and each containing a spiral staircase, are engraved with texts which are repeated both horizontally and vertically. The pinnacles crowning them are splendid examples of the surrealist imagination of Gaudí, and are covered in multi-coloured glazed vitreous mosaics and crowned by spectacular crosses. After Gaudí's death, worked continued, following his designs, and in 1987 the sculptor Josep Maria Subirachs began work on the images of the Passion façade which have incited some controversy. This has prompted much debate, with some asserting that it would be better to leave things as they are so as not to lose the essence of Gaudí's creation, whilst others argue that the cathedral should be finished, just as they were in medieval times, in spite of the death of the original architect. Beneath the four towers of the "Front of the Passion" is the **Museum of the Sagrada Família**, which contains an exhibition showing the history of the site.

Gaudí Avenue (7) begins at the junction of Marina Street and Provença Street. It was constructed only recently to afford a view of the Sagrada

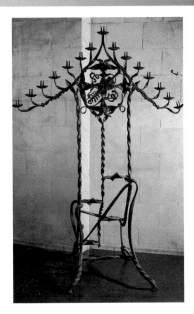

Fifteen candle candelabra used for Easter ceremonies, the work of Gaudí.

Gaudí Avenue.

Hospital de la Santa Creu i Sant Pau.

Família and the Hospital de Sant Pau. It was converted into a pedestrian area according to plans drawn up by Màrius Quintana in 1985, and now has an underground car park and a central promenade similar to the Rambla. It also features Modernist lamp-posts, designed by Pere Falqués, formerly emplaced at the Cinc d'Oros (the junction of Passeig de Gràcia and Diagonal Avenue).

At the end is a huge building which is also one of the most representative of Catalan Modernist architecture: the **Hospital de la Santa Creu i Sant Pau (8)**. The hospital occupies, 145,500 square metres, the equivalent of nine blocks in Barcelona's Eixample district. It was built thanks to the generosity of a Catalan banker, resident in Paris, who left four million pesetas to the city to be used for the purpose. The hospital was built in 1901 by the architect Lluís Domènech i Montaner who, in order to show his disgust with the grid-like pattern of the Cerdà Plan, oriented the buildings in diagonal opposition to the new district. The design included the creation of 46 small pavilions devoted to different medical specialisations, joined by underground corridors so that patients could be transferred without having go outside, and surrounded by what was originally conceived as a large gardened area. Over the main entrance to the central pavilion situated in one corner of the site, is a large clock. Over the years, this pavilion, the most characteristic element in Domènech i Montaner's architectural masterpiece, has become an identifying symbol of the hospital. It consists of a semi-basement and three storeys, with a central body and two wings at rightangles to it. The ward pavilions follow much the same pattern, being made up of a room with eight pointed arches, communicating with the different dependencies on the one hand and the isolation ward on the other. There is a profusion of floral ornamentation in the building, and the materials used, stone, mosaic, brick, ceramic and, to a lesser degree, marble and iron, are all left uncovered. A pavilion for tuberculosis patients was added in 1936 and in 1961 the seven-storey building housing the Puigvert Foundation was built. In Cartagena Street, going around

the Hospital de Sant Pau, we come to Ronda del Guinardó, an important traffic artery. Turning left, we arrive at the **Les Aigües Park and Tower (9)**. This is a small, leafy park which originally belonged to the water company and was used as the district reservoir. The Moorish-style tower was constructed in 1890 by master builder Enric Figueras to serve as the residence of a foreign technician hire by the company, though it was not, in the end, ever inhabited. It was restored in 1989.

We end this itinerary with a visit to the **Park Güell (10)**, 150 metres above sea level on Mount Carmel. Eusebi Güell had the original idea, commissioning Gaudí with its execution. The initial plan was to build an English-style garden city with 60 one-family houses. In the end, only two of these were built, the

Main steps in Güell Park.

Entrance pavilions, Güell Park.

The so-called Room of One Hundred Columns.

The dragon of Güell Park.

The undulating bench.

architect himself living in one until he moved to the Sagrada Família. In this park, Gaudí's creative genius achieved an architectural space in perfect communion and harmony with nature. At the main entrance to the park are two pavilions marking the end of the encircling wall. The grilles and iron gate are not original, but came from the gardens of Vicens house, also by Gaudí. Close to the park entrance is a wide double staircase with, at the meeting-point of the two sections, small spaces with waterfalls and sculptures, including a colourful mosaic-covered dragon which, though small, has become a symbol of the park.

The steps lead up to what was originally planned to be a 100-columned chamber (only 84 of these Doric-inspired, slightly inclining columns were finally built) where the market was to have been placed. The columns support spherical domes, and above the chamber is the huge circular main square surrounding by an undulating bench. This is covered by a mosaic of glazed ceramic pieces to make a massive Impressionist collage. In order to achieve the anatomical shape of the bench, Gaudí seated a nude worker in plaster, obtaining a cast of the profile which he then used for the entire bench. The great circular terrace was designed to collect rainwater, which would run down the columns to a huge 12,000 m^3 tank under the chamber.

Particularly interesting is the **Gaudí House and Museum**, where the architect lived from 1906 to 1926. The museum contains furniture designed by Gaudí as well as some of his personal effects. Park Güell was declared Patrimony of Humanity by UNESCO in 1984.

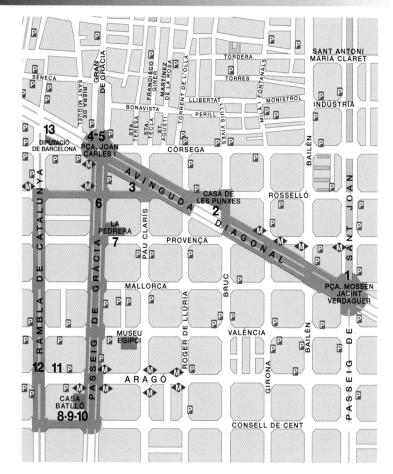

ITINERARY 5: (***) (A)

The route we suggest for this fifth itinerary will bring us into contact with some of the most representative examples of Modernist art and architecture in Barcelona and at the same time enable us to discover the modern-day heart of the city in one of its most active comercial and business centres.

1.- Mossèn Jacint Verdaguer Square (*) 2.- House of the Punxes (***) 3.- Quadras House (**) 4.- Joan Carles I Square (*) 5.- The Obelisk (*) 6.- Passeig de Gràcia (**) 7.- Milà House, "La Pedrera" (***) 8.- Lleó Morera House (***) 9.- Amatller House (***) 10.-Batlló House (***) 11.- The Antoni Tàpies Foundation (**) 12.- Rambla de Catalunya (**) 13.- Serra House or The Barcelona Diputation (**).

The route departs from **Mossèn Cinto Verdaguer Square (1)** which marks the meeting point between Diagonal Avenue and Passeig de Sant Joan. Here you can find the monument dedicated to the poet. It is the work of the architect Josep M. Pericas and was inaugurated in 1924. The monument is circular with a large column in the centre which supports the statue of the poet. It is surrounded by a stone wall decorated with reliefs and a small garden. The sculptural groups, which represent Verdaguer and epic poetry in both its mystic and popular form, are the work of Joan Borrell Nicolau, while the reliefs found on the lower part showing themes from "L'Atlàntida" (Verdaguer's masterpiece) were produced by the brother and sister team of Miquel and Llúcia Oslé.

Leaving this monument behind and continuing up the Diagonal avenue we arrive at the **House of the Punxes (2)** which

Mossèn Cinto Verdaguer Square.
House of the Punxes.

Comalat House, in Diagonal Avenue next to Pau Claris Street.

Quadras House.

forms a block of irregular buildings flanked by the above mentioned avenue and the streets Rosselló, Roger de Llúria and Bruc. The building was given this name after the sharp points which crown its turrets and give it a certain feel of a Nordic castle. The architect Josep Puig i Cadalfach was in charge of the construction of these three buildings, intended as private dwellings, between the years 1903 and 1905. The building has six facades decorated with motifs derived from the Northern Gothic style which coexist with others taken from the Spanish Plateresque. With the exception of the ground floor, which is faced with simple stone, the rest of the building is made of brick and covered with stone-carved sculptural motifs, glazed or coloured ceramic and wrought ironwork. The circular turrets, which finish in a point, rise up out of each of the six corners providing a harmonious enclosure. The turret corresponding to the corner which faces La Diagonal stands out from the rest both for its skylight and the fact that it is the highest. Particularly noteworthy are the panels found in the centre of each of the facades, which are decorated with floral, heraldic and feminine themes. In one of them, Cadalfach made evident the feelings for Catalan nationalism by including the inscription which reads "Saint Jordi, Patron Saint of Catalonia, return our freedom to us". The building Casa de les Punxes, which involved the collaboration of Alfons Juyol in the sculptural elements and Manuel Ballarín in the wrought ironwork, was declared a Historical-Artistic Monument of National Interest in 1976.

If we cross over the road to the other side of Diagonal, we can appreciate an unusual building known by the name of **Quadras House (3)** which can be found

Night view of Passeig de Gràcia.

Robert Palace.

at number 373. It is a palace constructed in 1904 when a building of rented accommodation was converted into a residence for Baron Quadras. The building is reminiscent of the Gothic palaces found in Barcelona. It has a central patio from which rises a flight of stairs which leads to the first floor. Here various rooms can be found which receive natural light from the openings in the facade. The building richly decorated and there is an undeniably Gothic feel to some of its nooks and crannys. The back of the building, which looks into Rosselló Street, contains hardly any decorative elements at all and was built over the first floor of the existing building which provided rented accommodation. The Quadras House, is the headquarters of the **Music Museum**, currently closed for improvements, and houses an important collection of musical instruments throughout the ages.

Remaining in Diagonal, but continuing on a few metres from this building, we find **Joan Carles I Square (4)** slotted into the crossroads traditionally known as the "Cinc d'Oros". The intersection between Passeig de Gràcia and Diagonal was given this name because it was once lit up by five Modernist lampposts which can now be found in the Gaudí Avenue. In the centre of the square there is an **Obelisk (5)** depicting "Victory", the work of Frederic Marès. On

Fuster House, next to the small square Els Jardinets de Gràcia.

one side there is the **Robert Palace**, used for seasonal exhibitions with pleasant gardens at the rear.

Looking up from this square towards the mountains lies the boundary of the friendly **district of Gràcia** which begins at the small square known as Els Jardinets and contains many examples of Modernist and "Noucentiste" architecture. The two most important streets are Gran de Gràcia and Travessera de Gràcia, but the visitor would do best to visit the squares (Diamant, del Sol, Rius and Taulet, Raspall or Virreina) along with the Santa Isabel and Llibertat markets. However, if from Joan Carles I Square we start to move towards the sea, we will enter into the **Passeig de Gràcia (6)** which has been converted into a veritable "museum" of Catalan Modernism. This was the first road which was set

out between the old city and the emerging district of Gràcia. Houses and palaces were constructed along both sides of the avenue including "La Pedrera" and the buildings found in the "Manzana de la Discordia" ("Apple, or Block, of Discord"). This name was given to the group of buildings because of the contrast in styles presented by the adjoining row of facades.

It is here that we can admire one of the masterpieces produced by Antoni Gaudí and which broke the mould of architectonic convention and was to become a decisive symbol of the artist's personal style. We refer to the **Milà House (7)** popularly known as **"La Pedrera"**. It was built between the years 1905 and 1910. When the project was begun the architect commissioned the plaster worker Beltrán to make a mock-up which served

Milà House, "La Pedrera".

Casa Milà roof.

Detail of the facade of Milà House.

Milà House: entrance stairway leading to the main floor.

as a starting point for the original plan, although it was later submitted to numerous changes. Originally the genius Gaudí conceived of the building as a monumental pedestal intended to support the image of the Virgin of the Rosary, which would have been accompanied by the surrounding figures of Saint Michael and Saint Gabriel. However the events of the "Setmana Tràgica" in 1909 forced the owner to reconsider his original intentions. Fearing that the image could be considered provocative, it was never even sculpted. The Milà House is formed by two detached buildings each with their own entrance way. They are joined together and their five floors are organised around two large interior patios (one circular in form and the other elliptical). The facade is an excellent example of Gaudí's creative capacity. Here the pieces of wrought iron, the work of Josep Maria Jujol, contrast with the white stone which was brought from Vilafranca del Penedès. The undulating curves of the building are formed out of self supporting stones which are joined to the rest of the building by curved butresses giving a feeling of weightlessness and movement to the construction. The interior of the building contains small ventilation shafts but has no communal staircase. Access to the different flats is obtained by using either the lift or the service stairway. However, it is on the roof terrace where you can find the most daring artistic forms: chimney and ventilation turrets dressed in white marble, fancy brickwork and the sides of bottles form abstract figurations which bring to mind the works of the Surrealists. At the same time the roofing takes on different forms derived from marine flora and fauna. In 1969 the building was declared a Historical-Artistic Monument of National Interest and in 1984 UNESCO listed it in the catalogue of human patrimony.

In 1986 the building was restored by the Fundació de la Caixa de Catalunya that now uses it as its headquarters using the first floor as an exhibition room and the dormer windows in the space dedicated to the work of Gaudí known as **"Espai Gaudí"**. Since 1999 you can visit one of the floors of the building, decorated in accordance with the tastes of the period when it was built.

Very close to Passeig de Gràcia, València Street 284, you can find the **Barcelona Museum of Egyptology**, which dates to 1993 and holds more than 600 objects belonging to the Jordi Clos Egyptian Archaeological Collection. Here, one can delve deeper into one of the most fascinating cultures. The museum is organised into different ambiences: "The

Lleó Morera House.

Pharaoh", "Private Lives", "Daily Life", "Religious Beliefs and Funeral Rites", and "The Religious Universe". Regarding the objects on display, one particularly important piece is an exact replica of the Rossetta stone which is a key document for deciphering hieroglyphics.

A little further down we arrive at the Mançana de la Discòrdia. One of the buildings which makes up this nucleus is the **Lleò Morera House (8)**, built by Domènech i Montaner in 1905 and made up of a ground floor, four floors above and a roof terrace. The exterior facade is peopled by numerous scuptural elements and is crowned by a small niche which was destroyed during one of the confrontations with the Republican group in 1937 but was restored by Oscar Tusquets and Carles Díaz during the eighties. The stained glass windows,

the mosaics, the floor tiles and all the decorative elements in general provide an extensive example of the Modernist floral style. In the interior, the hallway, staircase and lift are all worth visiting since they provide us with a fine example of a typical middle class dwelling.

The oldest building found in this nucleus of architectural merit is the **Amatller House (9)** built by Puig i Cadalfach between 1890 and 1900 over an earlier construction. It has a polycrome facade finished with a curious scaling effect reminiscent of architectural elements found in foreign parts. The rest of the facade has a Neo-gothic feel. The ground floor has a gallery with six low arches flanked by two entrance doors. The balcony which presides over the first floor is formed by a remarkable design of wrought ironwork. At the next level the balconies have a

Amatller House and Batlló House.

Cornice in Batlló House.

connopial feel and the windows are placed in pairs. On the third floor, the facade has a long gallery formed by low arches similar to those of the ground floor. At higher levels the windows are formed by separate connopial arches. The entrance hall displays various relief scuptures amongst which can be seen various scenes showing allegorical subjects relating to the fine arts and Saint George attacking the dragon. In 1976 the building was listed as a Historic-Artistic monument of National Interest.

Completing the series of outstanding buildings which comprise this nucleus, we come to the **Batllò House (10)** situated at number 43 in Passeig de Gràcia. The original building was renovated by Gaudí who was commissioned by the textile industrialist Josep Batlló. The building can be easily identified by the sculptural play of its balconies found on the facade. Their undulating form is quite remarkable and on occasion they have been identified as an expression of the movement associated with the submarine world. The steeply sloped roof hides and attic and it is topped by a circular turret on which stand out in golden letters and anagram of the words "Jesus, Mary and Joseph" and a four- armed cross. In the undulating form of the roof a representation of the dragon killed by Saint George can be seen. Inside the building the floor tiles and the glazed ceramic stones found on the stairway change colour and tone as you move upwards. Each floor and each unit maintains its own unique relationship with the overall form and design of the stairwell. The banister reminds us of the backbone and tail

Antoni Tàpies Foundation.

of the dragon. The building was also declared a Historical-Artistic Monument of National Interest in 1969.

We will leave the Batlló House to go on to an important centre of modern art which can be found at number 225 Aragó Street (between the Rambla de Catalunya and Passeig de Gràcia). Once the home of the publishing company Montaner i Simó, it nowadays houses the **Antoni Tàpies Foundation (11)**. The building was constructed in 1888 by Domènech i Montaner and it is included within the Catalan Modernist style. Tàpies was born in Barcelona in 1923. He abandoned his studies in law in order to dedicate more time to his pictoral and literary interests. Always controversial, his works are concerned with the renovation of plastic forms in accordance with contemporary trends. His paintings are inspired by everyday materials and objects, which also form the basis for the his sculptural - pictoric murals. The Foundation was set up by the artist himself in 1984 to promote the study of modern art and provide a place for exhibitions. It opened to the public in 1990. The facade boasts a metal roof which was intended to soften the difference in level with the adjoining buildings. However, Tàpies saw the opportunity to create another work of art and added a wire sculpture titled "Núvol i Cadira" (Cloud and Chair). The interior of the building reveals an innovative design: the space is distributed in a rational yet harmonious way and the original purpose of the building has very much been taken into consideration.

The **Rambla de Catalunya (12)**, which runs alongside the Foundation for Modern Art, is a continuation of the traditional Rambla as it leads upwards towards the mountains. For decades it has been one of the most elegant and welcoming roads in all the city. From top to bottom you can find boutiques and jewellery shops along with more up to date businesses. The terrace cafes, set up by the numerous bars, cafes and restaurants, are another traditional feature adorning the Rambla. Famous for containing numerous cinemas, the street is a meeting place, particularly in summer, for a large number of people who want to enjoy the Barcelona nightlife. Amongst many exceptional buildings is the **Farmàcia J. de Bolós** (at number 77) a Catalan Modernist work, and the **Serra House (13)**, present day home to Barcelona's Diputació or Provincial Council. The building was built between 1903 and 1908 by Josep Puig i Caldafach. It was originally designed as a small palace for one family with an adjoining garden behind it. A cylindrical turret is used to unite the two wings of the building. The construction reveals a combination of Gothic, Mudejar, Renaissance and Plateresque styles and is attached to a recently constructed building of modern design.

Rambla de Catalunya.

Serra House.

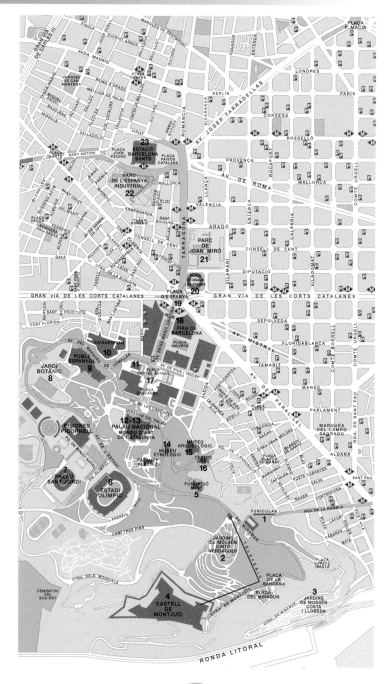

ITINERARY VI: (M AND A)

The following route brings us into contact with another of the city's vibrant cen-tres: Montjuïc and the area that surrounds it. Home to important cultural, sport-ing and commercial events, it possesses the charm of a mountain found in the heart of the city and close to the sea.

1.- Montjuïc Cablecar (*) 2.- Jacint Verdaguer Gardens (*) 3.- Costa i Llobera Gardens (*) 4.- Montjuïc Castle (***) 5.- Joan Miró Foundation (***) 6.- Olympic Stadium (***) 7.- Palau Sant Jordi (***) 8.- Botanical Garden (*) 9 - Poble Espany-ol (**) - 10.- CaixaForum (**) 11.- Mies van de Rohe Pavilion (**) - 12.- Montjuïc National Palace (***) 13.- National Art Museum of Catalonia (***) 14.- Ethnolog-ical Museum (*) 15.- Archaeological Museum (**) 16.- Grec Theatre (**) 17.- Mon-tjuïc Fountains (**) 18.- Trade Fair (*) 19.- Espanya Square (**) 20.- Les Arenes Bullring (**) 21.- Joan Miró Park (**) 22.- Parc de l'Espanya Industrial (**) 23.- Sants Railway Station (*).

Montjuïc Cablecar (1) which unites the Paral·lel underground station with the mountain. It was set up in 1929 for the Universal Exhibition. Although it once functioned regularly for a considerable period of time it was not until 1991 that it was put into working order again. The latest repair work, motivated by the Olympic Games, involved the replace-ment of the old tram lines, the repair-ing of the tunnel which passes under Nou de la Rambla Street and the length-ening of the platforms. The number of passengers that the cable car is able to carry in an hour was increased from 1,200 to 8,500.

Mirador de l'Alcalde gardens, in Montjüic.

Monument dedicated to the "sardana".

At the end of the funicular there is a link with the **Cable railway**, which climbs to the foot of Montjuïc Castle. Between the two points, either on the way up or on the way down, lovers of wide open green spaces can delight in a relaxing stroll through a number of parks: the **Jacint Verdaguer Gardens (2)**, recognisable by the floral coat of arms of the city, which presides over the entrance; the **Sardana Square**, with its monument dedicated to this typical Catalan dance; the **Mirador de l'Alcalde Gardens**, with attractive views of the city, and the **Costa i Llobera Gardens (3)**, dedicated to the Mallorcan poet, which is one of the most important exotic gardens in the world. Covering an area of six hectares, it gives us the opportunity to view an astonishing number of subtropical plants, originating from a variety of places such as

America, Madagascar or South Africa. Because of its topographic qualities this terrain is suitable for the cultivation of plants originating from climates hotter than that of Barcelona.

At the summit of the mountain we come to **Montjuïc Castle (4)**, well worth a visit for its historical value. The building was constructed in the second half of the eighteenth century and had its antecedents in an earlier castle built in 30 days during the war of "The Reapers" in 1640. After the struggle, the fortress passed into Royal hands and in 1694 it underwent a programme of extension which turned it into a considerable bastion occupying the topmost part of the mountain and playing an important part in the War of Succession. At the end of the war, King Philip V ordered its partial destruction although it was

Montjüic Castle.

totally rebuilt between 1751 and 1779 under the orders of Juan Martín Cermeño, who recognised its military importance. With the reforms the castle acquired the form of a five-pointed star which it has maintained to this day. At the beginning of the nineteenth century the building was used to house Napoleonic troops and from 1810 it was turned into a prison. In 1960 the castle was handed over to the city and in the same year it was restored by the architect Joaquim Ros de Ramis and made ready to house the Military Museum, which contains a large number of bellic weaponary and clothing and a collection of military miniatures.

Continuing our descent along the Miramar avenue, we can halt at one of the city's most original centres for contemporary art, the **Joan Miró Foundation**

An old cannon, next to Montjüic Castle.

Montjüic cable railway.

Miró Foundation.

(5). The building was designed by Josep Lluís Sert, a friend of Miró himself, in the seventies. It is a rationalist construction with just one floor which is built around an interior patio. The different rooms which make up the building are illuminated from above and the entrance is dominated by a tower reminiscent of the old Catalan Gothic bell-towers. Set up by Joan Miró himself in 1971, the foundation has a joint purpose: it is concerned both with the study and understanding of the artist's work and with the furtherance of contemporary art. The **Jardí d'Escultures** (Sculpture garden) was created in the area surrounding the building and here you can find works by Tom Carr, Pep Duran, Gabriel, Pere Jaume and Enric Pladevall amongst others. One of the Foundation's most important acquisitions is the "Mercury Fountain" designed by Alexander Calder in 1937 for the Spanish pavilion at the Universal Exhibition in Paris. In 1977, the museum received a special prize from the European Commission when it was declared the best museum in the world for that year.

Taking Estadi avenue on the west side of Montjuïc, we come to the **Olympic Ring**, the site which housed some of the most important sports facilities built or rehabilitated for the Olympic games. Our starting point is the **Olympic Stadium (6)** which was built for the 1929 Universal Exhibition. Originally it occupied 66,000 square metres of which 20,000 were intended to be used as sports fields. During the Republic, Barcelona was a candidate for the 1936 Olympic Games (the contest was won by Berlin) and its main point in favour was the stadium, which at the time was the second largest after Wembley. In 1955 the Second Mediterranean Games were held here. Halfway through the sixties the building was abandoned and a

Olympic Stadium and Palau Sant Jordi.

Calatrava Tower.

Swimming pools Picornell and Botanical Gardens.

process of decline took over which continued until 1985 when a programme of reformation was started based on Barcelona's bid to host the 1992 Olympic Games. The project was developed by the architects Correa, Milà, Margarit and Buxadé in collaboration with the Italian Vittorio Gregotti. The work consisted in the creation of a completely new stadium whilst conserving the earlier Neoclassical facade. The stadium floor was lowered by 11 metres, new rows of seats were put in for 55,000 spectators and 150 metres of roofing was added.

Opposite is the main sports facility to be found in the Olympic Ring complex, namely the **Palau Sant Jordi (7)**. It was designed by the Japanese architect, Arata Isozaki, who employed the most advanced technology in constructing the building. To raise the impressive roof structure (over 13,500 square metres) he used the latest system of hydraulic towers. The sports palace can seat 17,000 spectators. Inaugurated in September 1990, the building was awarded the FAD prize for Architecture in the same, together with the nearby telecommunications tower, **Torre Calatrava**, have changed the architectural make-up of the city by adding a distinctly modern aspect to its overall appearance.

Structural alterations in preparation for the 1992 Olympics also included the **Bernat Picornell Swimming Pools**, where the high diving board competitions were held.

En route to the Spanish Village, a visit to the **Barcelona Institute-Botanical Gardens (8)** is a must. These gardens focus especially on flora from the five Mediterranean climate regions of the world and are laid out according to the origin of the different species and their ecological affinities.

By following the Marquès de Comillas avenue we arrive at the **Poble Espanyol (9)**, a group of buildings constructed between 1926 and 1928 for the Universal Exhibition. The original idea was to bring together in the form of a picturesque Spanish village a synthetic assembly of Spanish monuments representative of the architectural traditions apparent in the different regions of Spain. Amongst its most characteristic elements are the walls that surround it and the two entrance towers which were constructed to evoke the city of Avilla. The interior of the village is organised around a large central square which is surrounded by narrow streets with typical buildings from different Spanish towns. There are also houses, little shops and workshops displaying a variety of craftwork and souvenirs. Nowadays, the "Spanish Village" forms

an exciting part of Barcelona's nightlife, offering a wide variety of entertainment. Further along the Marquès de Comillas avenue we come to the **CaixaForum (10)**, a large cultural center, is located, inside the old modernist textile factory, Casa Ramona, a work by Puig i Cadafalch in 1908. Since its inaugu-

Poble Espanyol: Avila Towers and Plaça Major.

The CaixaForum Cultural Center.

Mies van der Rohe Pavilion.

ration in 2002, it has become one of the most visited art centres in the city. Its rooms house the contemporary art collection of La Caixa Foundation, the entity that manages the center, and the temporary exhibits of international renown. The building, which operated as a factory until 1929 and which since the forties served as stables for the police, has been reconstructed, respecting the material and the archi-

tecture of the original work. The exception is the entrance area of the centre, designed by Arata Isozaki, characterized by a glass and steel structure in the form of a large tree.

As we move on to our next stopping point, it is worth our while to pause at the **Mies van der Rohe Pavilion (11)**. The building was designed by the architect as the German pavilion for the Universal Exhibition held in 1929 and experts have described it as a "paradigm of modern architecture" because of the perfect harmony achieved between interior and exterior space.

Now we suggest a visit to one of the most important buildings in the city, the **Montjuïc National Palace (12)** which is located in the Mirador Square. Built to preside over the complex of buildings constructed for the 1929 Exhibi-

Oval Room in the National Palace.

tion, it is centred around a large hall of elliptical form and decorated with both Classical and Churrigueresque motifs. As for its exterior appearance, a large dome dominates the central facade and the whole thing is reminiscent of the works of Michelangelo. It is decorated with murals painted by Francec Galí. At each end there are two smaller domes and four towers typical of those found in Santiago de Compostela.

In 1934 the palace was converted into the home for the **National Art Museum of Catalonia (MNAC) (13)** and it houses a priceless collection of Romanesque, Gothic, Renaissance and Baroque art. Between the years of 1985 and 1996 ambitious improvements were made to the Palace and the Museum, which expanded its former size. The visitor will also find an excellent collection at the

Pantocrator (12th century), fragment from the central apse of St. Climent of Taüll Church (Lleida). MNAC.

"Virgin of the Counselors", by Lluís Dalmau (1445).
"The Vicarage", by Marià Fortuny. National Art Museum of Catalonia (MNAC).

Museum of Modern Art, initially situated in the Ciutadella Park and moved here in 2004. This collection represents the most important works by Catalan artists from the first half of the 19th century up until the 1930's, one of the most outstanding periods in the history of all aspects of Catalan art. Above all, the outstanding feature of the building's interior is the oval room, of great beauty, which is occasionally used as a concert hall.

Leaving the National Palace to our right, we take the Passeig de Santa Madrona which will bring us to the **Ethnological Museum (14)** established in 1948. The museum contains an important collection of objects pertaining to the indigenous populations of Africa, Australia, the Pacific Islands, Central and Southern America and various parts of Asia. Of particular interest are the Pre-Columbian pieces from Central America, the collection of Japanese handiwork, the religious sculptures for India and the masks and other exhibits from Africa and Nepal.

Museum of Ethnological.

At number 39 in the same street, we can find another museum worth visiting. We refer to the **Archaeological Museum (15)**, opened in 1935. The building is "Noucentista" in style and displays some interesting sculptural and ornamental elements covered in terracotta. On exhibit in the museum is a large collection of pieces representative of the different cultural traditions found in Catalonia and the Balearic Islands from Paleolithic times to the age of the Visigoths. There are also ceramics, mosaics and sculptures from Greek and Roman times.

Mercat de les Flors Theatre.

Ascending slightly again up the Passeig de l'Exposició, we arrive at the **Grec Theatre (16)**. Built in 1929, it was inspired by the Epidaurian model. It consists of a stage whose backdrop is formed by ivy covered rocks which once belonged to an old abandoned quarry. The stepped rows of seats form a semicircle like those found in ancient Greek theatres. Since the time it was opened until 1936 the place was hardly used (it was open for scarcely two weeks) and from then on it was closed until 1952.

Grec Theatre.

From this year on, various open air performances took place which gradually turned "El Grec" into a popular space. The setting up of the "Grec Theatre Season" re-established the place as one of the city's theatres.

Next we head towards the Espanya Square by Passeig de les Cascades. On the way we cross Lleida street, where we will see three more of the cities scenic sites: The **Mercat de les Flors**, installed in an old flower market and in which we highlight, on the interior, a cupola painted by Miquel Barceló; the **Lliure Theatre**, a classic theatre in the Gràcia district which in the year 2002 moved to the Agriculture Palace in the Trade Fair ground, and the **Palau d'Esports**, which is a regular venue for music concerts.

We come to Carles Buïgas Square which is named after the engineer who designed the **Montjuïc Illuminated Fountain (17)** popularly known as the "Magic Fountain". Since it started working in 1929, the fountain and other smaller ones have become one the principal attractions to be found on Montjuïc, thanks to the spectacular shows of light, water and music. Restored by its designer in 1955, the fountain serves as a portico to the entrance of the Palau Nacional. At night, nine beams of light, visible throughout the city, rise up from behind the building. In 1969, Carles Buïgas was honoured with the Gold Medal for Artistic Merit.

Barcelona is a city with a long tradition of organising trade and industrial fairs as a way of invigorating its economy. This resulted in the creation of a special area to house the principal trade fairs. In this the **Barcelona Trade Fair (18)** was born and developed. The land that

Montjüic's illuminated fountains.

Reina Maria Cristina Avenue and the site of Barcelona's Trade Fair Centre.

it occupies was the subject of urban development for the World Expo in 1929. Today this area comprises a total of thirteen exhibition centres and has been extended with others in the Zona Franca. Reina Maria Cristina avenue, flanked on both sides by the enormous buildings used to house the trade fairs, takes us to **Espanya Square (19)**. Circular in form, it has a tunnel which absorbs much of the surrounding traffic. In the centre there is an imposing fountain designed by Josep M. Jujol. It is made up of three large columns and other sculptural

The fountain in Espanya Square.

Les Arenes Bullring.

"Woman and Bird", by Joan Miró in Escorxador Park.

groups created by Blay, Llovet and the Oslés. At the far end of the square, two towers marking the entrance to the Reina Maria Cristina avenue can be seen. They were set up in 1929 and are the work of Ramón Reventós. On either side of them are the columned facades of the **Palau del Treball** and the **Palau de Comunicacions i Transports**.

On the other side of the square a building stands out for its contrast in style to those surrounding it. We refer to **"Les Arenes" Bullring (20)**, built between 1889 and 1900 by August Font. It is a circular building with a diameter of 52 metres and a seating capacity of 15,000. The decorative style takes its inspiration from Arabic motifs. For some years now the bullring has been in disuse, due to the absence of bullfights, although there are plans to transform it into a commercial and recreational centre.

Behind the bullring, and at the edge of the "Eixample" district, you can find the **Escorxador Park**, an extensive green area which occupies the land where the municipal slaughter house once stood. Its official name is the **Joan Miró Park**

(21). The park was opened in 1983. It is dominated by a large statue by the artist called "Woman and Bird", which is 22 metres high. It emerges out of a rectangular pool which stands on a raised and paved square. A walkway covered with a pergola leads from the square to a group of holm oak and pine trees which separate an area of palm trees and a playground.

Continuing our journey along Tarragona Street, we turn left at Mallorca Street. From here we enter the **Parc de l'Espanya Industrial (22)** which extends over five hectares and lies over the land previously occupied by the old Vapor Nou factory. The park was created as part of a project to open up spaces to the public in an area of the city that was particularly built up. At the same time it was included in the plans to reorganise the area that surrounds Sants railway station. The park contains bridges, ponds and some spectacular lampposts

Espanya Industrial Park and Sants railway station.

reminiscent of the old coastal lighthouses. Amongst the group of sculptures to be found in the park can be seen the "Gran Drac de Sant Jordi" which rises out of the waters of the lagoon. It is the work of Andrés Nagel.

In front of the Països Catalans Square lies **Sants Railway Station (23)** which together with the newly renovated France Railway Station deals with the majority of Barcelona's freight and passenger lines. The Barcelona-Sants hotel was built over the station in 1992 and gives direct access to the station below.

Modernist style ornamental finishing on a house near to Espanya Square.

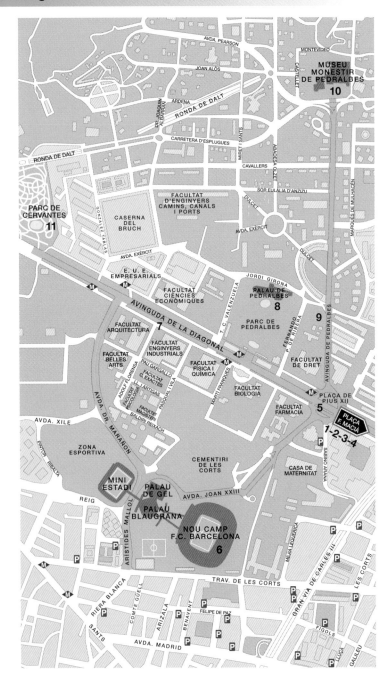

ITINERARY 7 (***) (M)

This itinerary takes us to the upper sections of the city, for the most part occupied by residential zones. This is the southern edge of Barcelona, the starting-point for the roads and motorways which connect it with the rest of Catalonia and Spain.

1.- Diagonal Avenue (**) 2.- Francesc Macià Square (*) 3.- Pau Casals Avenue (**) 4.- Atalaya, Trade Building, Illa Diagonal (*) 5.- Pius XII Square (*) 6.- Barcelona Football Club Stadium (***) 7.- Zona Universitària (*) 8.- Pedralbes' Palace (***) 9.- Güell Pavilions (***) 10.- Monastery of Pedralbes (***) 11.- Cervantes Park (**).

Diagonal Avenue (1) is, with Gran Via, one of the longest streets in Barcelona. It crosses the city diagonally from north to south from the sea, by the site of the Forum, to the exit at Zona Universitària. We begin this itinerary in one of the most prestigious squares in the city: **Francesc Macià Square (2)**, a cir-cular space whose centre is occupied by a garden and several small pools. All around are the seats of important companies and department stores such as El Corte Inglés, as well of well-known bars of long tradition (La Oca, for instance).

Various roads commence in the

Diagonal Avenue, the entrance stretch, south Barcelona.

Francesc Macià Square.

Banca building.

L'Illa Diagonal.

square. On the right is **Pau Casals Avenue (3)**, a tiny gardened "Rambla" leading to one of Barcelona's finest parks, **Turó Park**.

Retracing our steps along Diagonal, we will see a number of buildings worth pointing out on the way due to their modern architectural style. The high **Atalaya** building, for example, the seats of La Caixa and the **Trade Building (4)**, all on the left-hand side, four undulating constructions. More recent, the "Golden Block" is occupied by **L'Illa Diagonal**, with all the feaures of a high-rise building, but placed horizontally. This huge complex contains offices, a hotel and a large shopping centre.

At the junction with **Pius XII Square (5)**, we are faced with various options. To the left is Joan XXIII Avenue, leading to one of the most popular sights with visitors to the city, the "Camp Nou", or **Barcelona Football Club Stadium (6)**. The

The Trade Building, work of José Antonio Coderch and Manuel Valls in 1969

F.C. Barcelona football stadium known as "Camp Nou".

ground has a capacity of 120,000 and was opened in 1957. Despite its enormous size, it is rightly famous for the excellent view of the players, and it is considered one of the finest stadiums in the world. Its canopy, supported only by external pillars, is a remarkable construction.

Inside is the **Museu del Barça** (as the team is popularly known), with kits, pennants, photos and the many trophies won by this team, belonging to an entity thought of as "more than a club". The seat of the Fundació Barça, created to promote parallel activities, is also in the ground.

The complex also includes an ice rink, sports hall, mini-stadium, training pitches, a shop and a masia, one of the few such traditional houses existing in the city, which serves as a hostal for young players.

Returning once more to Diagonal Avenue, between Pedralbes Avenue and Doctor Marañón Avenue is the **Zona Universitària (University) (7)**, occupied by one of Barcelona's four such centres, created during the 1950s.

Turning right into Pedralbes Avenue we enter the district of the same name which, as well as being one of the city's most prestigious residential areas, also contains various palaces and such an important monument as the monastery. At Diagonal number 686 is the **Pedralbes' Palace (8)**. This palace

View of Zona Universitària.

Pedralbes' Palace

Monument dedicated to Gaudí and Miralles Estate porch, the work of Gaudí, near to the Güell Pavilions.

was constructed on land belonging to the Güell family as a residence for King Alfonso XIII.

Building began in 1921 under the direction of architects Eusebi Bona i Puig and Francesc de Paula Nebot. However, history took a drastic turn and, rather than by the king, the palace was inhabited first by the leaders of the Republic and later by General Franco. The Palau de Pedralbes was declared a Historic-Artistic Monument of National Interest in 1931, at the same time as it became property of the City Council. The structure consists of a central four-storey building flanked on either side by three-storey wings. Inside on the ground floor is the splendid throne room, the large dining room and the music room. The building contains many fine works of art. It has been open to the public since 1960, housing such collections as the **Ceramic Museum** and the **Decorative Arts Museum.**

Further along Pedralbes Avenue we come to the **Güell Pavilions (9)**, which stood at the main entrance to what was later converted into Pedralbes' Palace. The hand of Gaudí can be clearly seen in the doors, walls and entrance

Güell Pavilions: dragon on the entrance gate.

pavilions, all that remains of the tiny Güell palace.

The **Monastery of Pedralbes (10)** was constructed thanks to the efforts of Elisenda de Montcada, last wife of King Jaume II who, on learning that the king wished to be laid to rest elsewhere, next to his first wife, decided to build a monastery as her own last resting-place. When the king died, Elisenda moved to a house adjoining the monastery which, in acordance with her wishes, was destroyed on her death, with just a few ruins of it remaining today. The monastery began to be built in 1326 and was dedicated to the Virgin Mary and cared for by nuns of the Poor Clares order. Its rapid construction and the fact that it was inhabited by just one order of nuns contributed in great part to its unity of style. Its outstanding element are the splendid three-storey cloisters, built in Gothic style and considered to be amongst the most beautiful in the world. The church consists of a single nave with side chapels used, for the most part, as the resting place of noblemen and women, among them Elisenda de Montcada.

In recognition of its status as one of the jewels of Catalan Gothic architecture, in 1931 the Monastery of Pedralbes was declared a Historic-Artistic Monument of National Interest.

The chapterhouse of the monastery contains the **Museum of the Monastery of Pedralbes**, with a

Pedralbes' Monastery.

splendid collection of furniture, as well as paintings, altarpieces and carvings, mostly from the16th-17th centuries. Part of the nuns' dormitory area has also been converted into a room housing the Von **Thyssen-Bornemisza Collection** of works of art.

Though this reorganisation broke somewhat with the style of the rest of the monastery, still the space makes an excellent exhibition area and auditorium for classical music concerts.

We complete this itinerary almost at the exit from Barcelona, at the **Cervantes Park (11)** on Diagonal Avenue. This park was opened in 1965, its 87,665 square metres laid out by the architect Lluís Riudor i Carol. The outstanding feature here

Cervantes Park

is the marvellous rose garden, with a huge variety of types of rose, all with accompanying description. Scattered around the park are sculptures by Alfaro, Eulàlia Fàbregas de Sentmenat and J.D. de la Campa, as well as a monument to the poet Maragall, by his own son.

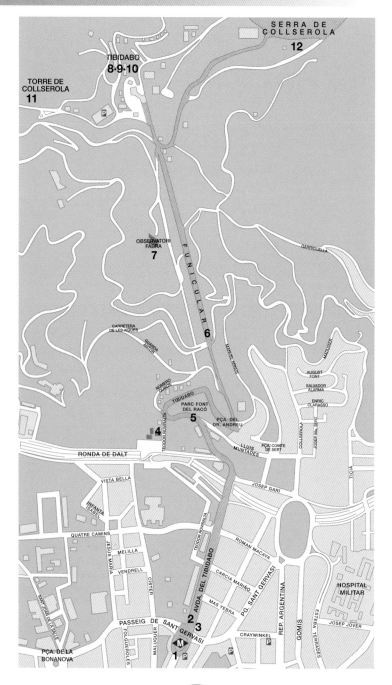

ITINERARY 8 (***) (M)

We propose in this itinerary a visit to Mount Tibidabo in the Serra de Collserola, starting out from John Kennedy Square, at the junction of Balmes Street and Passeig de Sant Gervasi.

1.- John F. Kennedy Square (*) 2.- Tibidabo Avenue (*) 3.- Blue Tram (**) 4. - Science Museum (**) 5.- Font del Racó Park (*) 6.- Funicular railway (*) 7.- Fabra Observatory (**) 8.- Expiatory Church of the Sacred Heart (**) 9.- Tibidabo Funfair (***) 10.- Automaton Museum (**) 11.- Collserola Tower (***) 12.- Serra de Collserola (*).

From the **John Kennedy Square (1)**, we will go up the mountain on one of the most picturesque of the means of transport in Barcelona, covering the distance from the bottom of **Tibidabo Avenue (2)** and the foot of the funicular railway on the **"Blue Tram" (3)**, a tramline dating back to the year 1901 and whose first stop was precisely here.

The tram was born of the illustrious Doctor Andreu's plan to urbanise the foothills of Tibidabo and convert the area into a residential zone, with a funfair at the summit reached by a tram and a funicular railway. The tram has witnessed many important historical events: in 1904, whilst visiting the city, King Alfonso XIII refused to

The Blue Tram.

Submarine outside the Science Museum.

Room in the Science Museum.

cés and Enric Sòria. The museum, which belongs to the Caixa Foundation, stands just beside one of the new rondes, ring roads built to facilitate traffic circulation in preparation for the 1992 Olympic Games. The museum is an ideal spot to spend a few hours having fun whilst learning some of the secrets of science. For this is not a place where the visitor has to be content with merely observing, but an interactive centre where he/she can take part in experiments and demonstrations given by the different exhibits. There are rooms dedicated to optics, the senses, waves, mechanics, new materials and biology (in the Living Planet room, where we can observe living beings and study their behaviour). There is also a special activ-

travel on it and travelled by car to the foot of the funicular railway. Finally, it was the only line to survive when the city's tramlines were closed down.

As we ascend the slopes of Tibidabo, we see on the left the building housing the **Science Museum (4)**, constructed at the beginning of the 20th century and rehabilitated by the architects Jordi Garity area for the very young, el *Clic dels Nens*. Other areas include the Planetarium, where we can submerge ourselves in the immensity of the Universe, and the temporary workshops and exhibitions, regularly changed to make a repeat visit at a later date all the more worthwhile. Other activities include schools programmes, courses, conferences and much more, all aimed at bringing science closer to the ordinary people of all ages and social conditions.

Font del Racó Park.

Tibidabo Funicular Railway.

At the end of Tibidabo Avenue is the **Font del Racó Park (5)**, a romantic garden commanding splendid views of the city and leading directly to Doctor Andreu Square, starting-point of the **Funicular railway (6)**. Inaugurated in 1901, this was the first such railway to be

Arnes House and unstaffed station of Tibidabo's funicular railway.

Fabra Observatory.

Ascending along Carretera del Tibidabo, we can now see the **Fabra Observatory (7)**, a Modernist building designed by Domènec i Estepà with the technical assessment of the astronomer Josep Comas i Solà. It was inaugurated in 1904 by Alfonso XIII and is property of the Barcelona Royal Academy of Arts and Sciences. The observatory consists of three sections, dedicated respectively to astronomy, seismology and meteorology. It forms part of the worldwide astrometric network, and is in fact one of its oldest members. The building is made up of an octagonal main body on which is mounted a revolving dome made of iron, which contains the telescope, and another rectangular section with a gable roof with a narrow opening for observation equipment.

built in Spain. The single line is 1,152 metres long and rises 275 metres in altitude. It was constructed by a Swiss company, and at first was popularly known as the "Funi", to the point where the Santiago Rusiñol once wrote "I went up *Tibi* on the *Funi*".

Church of the Sacred Heart and Tibidabo Funfair.

Church of the Sacred Heart.

Tibidabo Funfair and the city.

Crowning Mount Tibidabo is the **Expiatory Church of the Sacred Heart (8)**, a Neo-Gothic building commenced in 1902 by the architect Enric Sagnier, though not completed for another 60 years. The church features a monumental statue of Christ with open arms, the effect of his merciful gesture somewhat lost in the complex patterns formed by the communications towers surrounding it.

At the foot of this church is **Tibidabo Funfair (9)**, an enormous area full of fun and excitement for young and old alike. The history of the funfair goes back to the late-19th century, when Doctor Andreu founded the company Tibidabo, SA, with the aim of converting this part of the mountain into a garden city with a vast variety of leisure facilities. In execution of this plan, he installed many different attractions: firstly, the automatons, next the aerial railway, and so on. The funfair now occupies 70,000 square metres, having transformed Tibidabo into a veritable "magic mountain" where fantasy takes over from reality.

One of the principal attractions is the **Automaton Museum (10)**, housed in a Modernist building dating back to the early years of the 20th century. This museum contains a fascinating collection of mechanical dolls and machines.

Not far from the summit of Mount Tibidabo is the **Collserola Communications Tower (11)**, designed by the famous British architect

Norman Foster. This was built along with all the other important infra-structures with which the city was modernised in preparation for the 1992 Olympics.

At 288 metres, this is the highest tower in Spain and the fifth high-est in Europe. Its sophisticated design breaks the mould of con-ventional communications towers. It consists of a 4.5 metre diame-ter concrete shaft, a 38 metre high tubular steel mast and a 45 metre section of lattice. Before work began, the complete collection of coins commemorating the 1992 Olympics were buried at the base of the cylinder. Inside, it contains a number of systems which had previously been scattered over the Serra de Collserola.

Between the heights of 84 metres and 152 metres are 13 platforms for radar and other broadcasting and reception gear. The tenth plat-form has been reserved as a pub-lic gallery, at an altitude of over 550 metres above sea level, com-manding unbeatable views over the city.

The tower is built to withstand winds of up to 300 kilometres per hour. The support building is a two-storey construction, partly underground, over which gardens have been laid. In just a few years, the Collserola Communications Tower has become an emblematic symbol of the new, modern aspect of Barcelona.

The **Serra de Collserola (12)** is a huge nature reserve and important green belt for the city. Guided tours of the park can be made, allow-ing the visitor to identify the wide variety of vegetation of the zone.

Collserola tower.

Figueras House, or Bellesguard, the work of Gaudí, a private residence in Bellesguard Street, at the foot of Tibidabo.

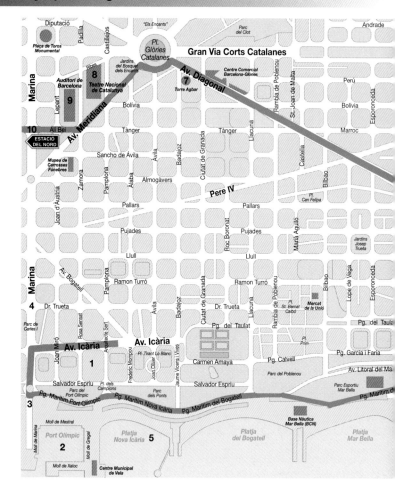

ITINERARIO 9: (**) (T)

In this last itinerary we propose a visit to the modern face of Barcelona. The Olympic Village, an area created on the occasion of the 1992 Olympic Games, next we come to the Forum Site, an area completely urbanized in 2004, and conclude the tour in Glòries Square, close to where there are also various works of recent construction.

1.- Olympic Village (**). 2.- Port Olympic (***). 3.- Hotel Arts and Mapfre Tower (**). 4.- Marina Street (*). 5.- Nova Icària, Bogatell and Mar Bella beaches (**). 6.- Forum Site 2004 (***). 7.- Agbar Tower (**). 8.- National Theatre of Catalonia (*). 9.- Barcelona Auditorium (*). 10.- North Station (*).

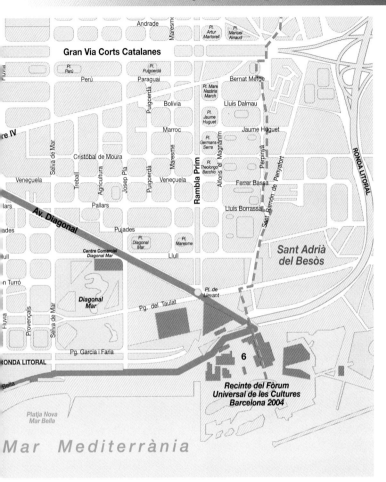

The area where the **Olympic Village (1)** is established replaces the old industrial zone of Poble Nou, which had become one of the most degraded districts in the city. As a result of Barcelona´s nomination to host the Olympic Games, this entire area was renovated: the existing factories were pulled down and a completely new small town was raised in its place, where the athletes stayed during the event, and which claims to be an urban model. Its construction was initiated at the start of a project by the architects Mackay, Martorell, Bohigas and Puigdomènech in 1985. The residential zone covers 50 hectares and contains 2,000 dwellings, their arrangement inspired by Ildefons Cerdà's design of the "Eixample" district, with straight roads and wide blocks of houses built around gardened areas, where the services are also located. One of its principal arter-

Icària Avenue.

ies is the **Icària Avenue**, where upon the central walkway original coverings were installed in 1992 designed by Enric Miralles and Carme Pinós. On the other hand, the Olympic Village also benefits from extensive landscaped areas, which together represent practically half the entire green zone of Barcelona, (more than 50 hectares, without including the two parks Montjuïc and Collserola). It has a 25-metre wide, two-kilometre long coastal promenade, parallel to which is the new **Litoral Park**, a park in three sections: Les Cascades, Port and Icària, green areas of varied vegetation and specially-designed facilities, adapting to the structure of the main thoroughfare, the Ronda del Litoral.

Port Olympic (2) was also created for the purpose of celebrating the 1992 Games, being the main centre for the sailing events. It is a modern port used today as much for nautical purposes, as for a civic recreational centre, with more that 40 restaurants and bars, as well as the Municipal Sailing Centre. Its eight hectares of protected waters contain moorings for 743 boats. It was designed by the team of Ramón de Clascà. In order to equip the port with a jetty which would be low enough not to be a visual obstacle but high enough to maintain calm conditions within the harbour, a semi-curved, scaled breakwater was constructed, which reduces storm impact and also contains seating areas.

Next to Port Olympic, are two buildings, of the same date, which have modified the outline of the city: namely the two skyscrapers **Hotel Arts** and **Mapfre Tower (3)**, which are the tallest in Barcelona, at 150 metres,

Port Olympic; Hotel Arts and Mapfre Tower.

though they are surpassed in height by the Collserola Telecommunications Tower. The **Hotel Arts** was built using the most advanced engineering systems. Designed by the American architect Bruce Graham, it is an enormous glass structure enveloped in a white metallic frame reminiscent of a child's building game. There are 44 storeys with 455 rooms and 29 apartments. The hotel also has an underground car park and ten meeting rooms, making it an important international congress centre. The area around the hotel is made up of a shopping centre and an extensive green area where you can see the **fish of golden reflections** designed by Frank Gehry. This is a gigantic bronze sculpture so large that you can see it from any point of Barcelona's seafront promenade, known as the Paseig Marítim.

The **Mapfre Tower** was designed by Iñigo Ortiz and Enrique León and is an office building with stainless steel and glass fronts. Its windows are slightly inclined towards the ground in order to avoid giving a feeling of vertigo and to allow a better from of the city from inside the building. The build-

Bogatell Beach.

ing is equipped with two-storey lifts to cope with peak demand, the first such system in Europe.

These two skyscrapers flank the beginning of **Marina Street (4)** a street which previously came to a halt some distance from the sea, unable to cross the railway lines, but which now reaches the port and forms a main communications artery between the Olympic Village and the city centre. We continue by the **Sea front Promenade** in a northerly direction. Restaurants and beach bars enliven this pleasant promenade, especially popular in good weather and runs alongside the **beaches Bogatell, Nova Icaria, Mar Bella and Nova Mar Bella (5)**. At the end of the promenade spreads out the **Forum Site 2004 (6)**.

The date for the 2004 Forum celebrated between May and September of 2004, for promoting cultural diver-

sity in the world, which this active city has wagered on, has also meant the renovation of an urban area where hardly anything existed before. Because of this, Barcelona has gained a new space of about 30 hectares next to the sea, between the district of Poble Nou and the Besòs River. There are essentially seven newly constructed installations prompted by the 2004 Forum: the **Forum Building**, the most emblematic due to its innovative design; the **CCIB or the International Convention Centre of Barcelona**, with capacity for 26,000 spectators; the **Park of Auditoriums**, which includes two open-air amphitheatres for 3,500 and 2,500 spectators; **the Plaça**, an extensive, 14-hectare esplanade with views of the sea, created as a large recreational area, **Pangea Island**, opposite the Park of Auditoriums and 60 m away from the coast, only accessible by swimming;

Aerial view of the Forum Site.

The Besós Tram.

a new **marina** with capacity for a thousand moorings, and the **Northeast Park**, a spacious garden that culminates in a 500-m long beach. Alongside the Forum Site a new hotel and residential area has been developed, together with a commercial centre, **Diagonal Mar**, which houses also a large cinema complex.

By means of the tram, inaugurated in 2004, or on foot, we cover the area north of Diagonal Avenue to arrive at **Glòries Square**. It is an important communications centre, next to which we find various newly constructed edifices, such as **Glòries Commercial Centre**, also equipped with cinemas, and the **Agbar Tower (7)**, an imposing construction 142 m high, designed by Jean Nouvel and completed in 2004. With 32 floors, 39,000 m² dedicated to office space and 9,000 m² to parking. It is the head office of the Agbar Group (Waters of Barcelona). From high up, the building enjoys a vantage point dominating the entire city. On the exterior, the building presents an attractive chromatic spectacle due to its cloak of tinted aluminium and translucent crystal.

Close by, in the Arts Square, two scenic locations have recently added to the already extensive selection of theatres and music halls in the city: the **National Theatre of Catalonia (8)**, the work of Ricardo Botill, which has three halls of different seating capacities: 900, 400 y 300 spectators, and the **Barcelona Auditorium**

(9), designed by Rafael Moneo and inaugurated in 1999, with a capacity to seat 2,200 spectators in the Symphonic Hall and 400 spectators in the Polivalente Hall.

Further on from the Auditorium, occupying the entire block between the two streets Nàpols and Sardenya, is the **North Station (10)**. The grounds of this former railway station have

The Agbar Tower and the Nacional Theatre of Catalonia.

Barcelona Auditorium.

now been converted into an important coach station, whilst of the original building the huge vestibule and front have been conserved, along with the semi-spherical glass roof. To the south is a fine green park featuring various sculptures by the American artist Beverly Pepper. The park was designed by the Catalan architects Carme Fiol and Andreu Arriola.

North Station.

ALPHABETICAL INDEX OF MONUMENTS AND POINTS OF INTEREST:

CONTENTS

Introduction...2

How to use this guide...3

Historic background 4

ITINERARIES:

EDITORIAL ESCUDO DE ORO, S.A.
I.S.B.N. 84-378-2285-8
Printed by FISA - Escudo de Oro, S.A.
Legal Dep. B. 30654-2004

Protegemos el bosque; papel procedente de cultivos forestales controlados
Wir schützen den Wald. Papier aus kontrollierten Forsten.
We protect our forests. The paper used comes from controlled forestry plantations
Nous sauvegardons la forêt: papier provenant de cultures forestières contrôlées